# FOREWORD

Dear Sunseeker

As the Acting Commissioner for the Department of Tourism for the United States Virgin Islands, I am very pleased to welcome 'Sunseekers Guide to the U.S. Virgin Islands'. The Department of Tourism feels this guidebook will be a valuable tool in planning your trip to our beautiful islands. I am very grateful to Moorland Publishing for adding the U.S. Virgin Islands to their series of Caribbean guidebooks. The 'Sunseekers Guide' has been approved by the Department of Tourism, so I assure you that Moorland Publishing is providing you with the most factual and current information available on the U.S. Virgin Islands.

I am also indeed grateful to its writer and editor, Don Philpott, who has thoroughly researched every area of St. Croix, St. Thomas and St. John. He has covered areas that would be of interest to all of our visitors, from taking a stroll in our historic districts to yachting about our tranquil seas and cays. You'll discover that no other island compares to the U.S. Virgin Islands' history, people, attractions, and its adoring views.

When you arrive, you'll immediately realize that you have landed in the most popular cruise ship port in the eastern Caribbean. The pristine beaches and views are so inviting, you can see why Christopher Columbus was enticed to land on these shores more than 500 hundred years ago. Besides its early inhabitants of Ciboney, Arawak, and Carib Indians, and of course its band of pirates, countries from all over the world have been charmed by our islands. Seven flags have flown above the U.S. Virgin Islands: Spain, England, Holland, France, Knights of Malta, Denmark and the United States. Any wonder why the people of the U.S. Virgin Islands are so diverse in origin and in culture.

It may have all started out to be a military advantage for the United States to purchase the U.S. Virgin Islands in 1917, but it has grown to be a trilogy of beauty, warmth, and adventure. As you trek where thousands have before, take some time to contemplate what the early colonists may have felt while exploring our new world. You'll see our bounty is rich with unmeasurable wealth — an abundance that has been enhanced by your presence.

See you soon in America's Paradise,

Dr. David L. Edgell, Acting Commissioner

## CARIBBEAN SUNSEEKERS
# U.S. Virgin Islands

Don Philpott

**PASSPORT BOOKS**
a division of *NTC Publishing Group*
Lincolnwood, Illinois USA

Published by Passport Books,
a division of NTC Publishing Group,
4255 West Touhy Avenue,
Lincolnwood (Chicago), Illinois
60646 – 1975 USA

ISBN 0 8442 4943-2

© Don Philpott 1996

All rights reserved. No part of this publication may be reproduced, stored in a retrieval system, or transmitted in any form or by any means, electronic, mechanical, photocopying, recording or otherwise without the prior permission of the publishers.

Library of Congress Catalog Card Number:
95-74808

Color origination by: Reed Reprographics, Ipswich, England
Printed in Hong Kong: by Wing King Tong Co Ltd

ACKNOWLEDGMENTS:

Gloria Gumbs and Heather L. Carty of the US Virgin Islands Division of Tourism, William F. Cissel, of the National Park Service, St. Croix, Mike Gaston, Secret Harbour Beach Resort, St. Thomas, Jill McCall of Coral World, St. Thomas, Diane Ammodt and Marston Winkles of the Grand Palazzo Hotel, St. Thomas, Randy Doty of Bolongo Club Everything, Elizabeth A. Armstrong of The Buccaneer, St. Croix, Martin Nicholson of Caneel Bay, and Torre Newman and all at Hotel 1829, and John Abraham, Cool Running Taxis, St. John.

PICTURE CREDITS:
Front cover: Back cover: page 2/3 Near The Buccaneer, St. Croix.
All photos are from the MPC Picture Collection except:
2,3 Appartment balcony, Cottage Point, Caneel Bay (Caneel Bay, A Rosewood Resort)
7, 11, 23, 54/55 Peter Martin Associates
15, 75 Coral World Marine Park, St. Thomas (Blazing Photos).

**Please note** that in September 1995, parts of the US Virgin Islands were badly damaged by Hurricane Marilyn

### DISCLAIMER

While every care has been taken to ensure that the information in this book is as accurate as possible at the time of publication, the publishers and author accept no responsibility for any loss, injury or inconvenience sustained by anyone using this book.

Your trip to the Caribbean should be a happy one, but certain activities such as water sports should be approached with care and under proper supervision when appropriate. It is also in your own interests to check locally about flora and fauna that it is best to avoid.

# Contents

| | |
|---|---|
| **Foreword** | **1** |

**Before You Go**    **7**
- Getting to US Virgin Islands   7
- When To Go   9
- Geography   9
- History   13
  - St. Thomas   16
  - St. John   17
  - St. Croix   20
- Weather   24
- The People   25
- Culture   26
- Economy   28
- Administration   29
- Flora and Fauna   30
- Food and Drink   41

**Touring & Exploring the US Virgin Islands**   **46**
- ***St. Thomas***   48
  - The Western Half Of The Island   68
  - The Eastern Half Of The Island   72
- ***St. John***   80
  - Cruz Bay   81
  - An Island Tour   85
  - Park Trails   93
- ***St. Croix***   100
  - Christiansted   101
  - The Western Tour   110
  - Frederiksted   115
  - The Eastern Tour   124

**Traveller's Tips**   **130**

**Feature Boxes**
- Sunseeker Hot Spots   10
- Beaches & Tanning Safely   14
- Shopping   18
- A Note Of Warning: The Manchineel   34
- Getting Around St. Thomas   50
- Getting Around St. John   83
- Getting Around St. Croix   107
- Salt River National Park   111

**Eating Out**
- ***St. Thomas***   65
  - In & Around Charlotte Amalie   65
  - On the West Of The Island   70
  - On the East Of The Island   77
- ***St. John***   97
- ***St. Croix***   100
  - In & Around Christiansted   108
  - On the Western Tour   121
  - On the Eastern Tour   129

**Index**   **158**

## KEY TO SYMBOLS USED IN TEXT MARGIN AND ON MAPS

- 🚶 Recommended walks
- 🐟 Aquatic interest
- ✳ Other place of interest
- 🏖 Beach
- 🦌 Nature Reserve/Animal interest
- 🌼 Garden
- 🏛 Museum
- ⛪ Church/Ecclesiastical site
- 🏢 Building of interest
- ⛵ Water Sports
- 🏞 Beautiful view/Scenery, Natural phenomenon
- 🐦 Birdlife
- ✈ Airport
- 🌳 Parkland
- 🏰 Castle/Fort

## KEY TO MAPS

- ——— Main Routes (Surfaced)
- ——— Secondary Routes
- - - - - - Ferry Route
- ▮ Town/Village
- ～ River

## HOW TO USE THIS GUIDE

Enjoying as much sun and fun on a vacation is everyone's dream. *Caribbean Sunseekers: US Virgin Islands* will help to make this dream come true. Your guide has been designed in three easy to use sections.
'Before You Go' is packed with detailed information on the island, its history, geography, people, culture, food and much more. 'Touring and Exploring US Virgin Islands' is a comprehensive itinerary covering each islands with a series of useful and practical motoring or walking tours. Many places are off the beaten track and not on the usual tourist circuit. 'Traveller's Tips' arranged in alphabetical order for easy reference, lists practical information and useful advice to help you plan your vacation before you go and while you are there.
Distinctive margin symbols in the text and on maps, plus places to visit highlighted in bold enable the reader to find the most interesting places with ease.

# Before You Go

The US Virgin Islands are a year-round tropical playground with near perfect weather, more than 200 miles (322km) of beautiful palm-fringed sandy beaches, warm surf, crystal clear aquamarine seas, coral reefs and spectacular scenery. The offshore waters offer world-class diving, game fishing and yachting. Each of the islands is different and has its own charms and attractions. There are historic buildings, traditional villages and modern luxury resorts, a wealth of land and water-based sporting opportunities and a wonderful cuisine to enjoy.

**GETTING THERE:**
By Air - There are international airports on both St. Thomas and St. Croix and both receive scheduled services.

From the US American Airlines fly direct from Miami and New

*Romantic days on St Thomas at the Sapphire Beach Resort*

York to St. Thomas, and non stop from Miami to St. Croix. They also fly from several US cities to their Caribbean hub at San Juan on Puerto Rico. Carnival Airlines fly non-stop from Fort Lauderdale, New York, Miami and Newark to San Juan and connect with commuter airlines to both St. Thomas and St. Croix.

Continental Airlines fly non-stop from Newark to St. Thomas and have several connecting flights from other US cities in Newark. Delta Airlines fly from Atlanta to St. Thomas and then on to St. Croix, with connecting services in Atlanta. Trans World Airlines fly direct from New York, St. Louis and Miami to San Juan with connecting commuter flights to St. Croix and St. Thomas, United Airlines fly from Chicago to San Juan to connect with commuter flights to the Virgin Islands, and US Air fly non-stop from Baltimore to St. Thomas and Philadelphia to San Juan for connecting flights to both St. Thomas and St. Croix. There are also many other flights from other US airports via San Juan in Puerto Rico, where there are a number of commuter flights to St. Thomas and St. Croix provided by American Eagle, LIAT, Caribair, Air Anguilla, Air St. Thomas, Air Puerto Rico, Eastern Metro Express and Aero Virgin Islands.

From the UK and Europe: There are no direct flights but you can fly British Airways to San Juan or Antigua, and then catch one of the many connecting flights, or fly to Miami to make a connection. Lufthansa fly from Frankfurt to San Juan, and Iberia from Madrid.

From other Caribbean Islands: LIAT offers scheduled services from St. Croix and St. Thomas to Antigua, Barbados, Dominica, Grenada, Guadeloupe, Martinique, Montserrat, Port of Spain, St. Kitts, St. Lucia, St. Maarten and St. Vincent, and additionally from St. Thomas to Anguilla, Barbuda, Caracas and Nevis. Air British Virgin Islands (Air BVI) fly between St. Thomas and Tortola and Virgin Gorda, and Eastern Metro Express fly between St. Thomas and Antigua, St. Kitts and St. Maarten.

**By sea**: There are regular ferries between St. Thomas and Tortola in the British Virgin Islands. The crossing takes about an hour.

Up to 1,000 cruise ships a year visit the islands, and the West India Company Dock in St. Thomas is the most popular cruise port in the Caribbean. St. Croix, with its modern $15 million (£6 million) cruise port, is also hugely popular.

Almost all the major cruise lines visit St. Thomas and St. Croix including American Canadian Line, Carnival Cruise Lines, Chandris Fantasy Cruises, Clipper Cruise Line, Commodore Cruise Line, Costa Cruises, Cunard, Epirotiki Line, Exploration Cruise Line, Holland America Line, Home Lines, Norwegian Caribbean Lines, Ocean Cruise Lines, Paquet French Cruises, Princess Cruises, Royal Caribbean Cruises, Royal Viking Line, Sitmar Cruises and Sun Line.

There are also regular ferries between Red Hook, St. Thomas to Cruz Bay, St. John (20 minutes), from Charlotte Amalie to Cruz Bay (45 minutes) and Water Island.

## WHEN TO GO

High season, and therefore, higher prices, is from mid-December to mid-April when people from colder climates look for the sun, but any time of the year is a good time to visit, and the tourists do arrive year round by air and cruise ship. The temperatures do not vary greatly from month to month, and while there is more rainfall in the second half of the year, the downpours while heavy, do not often last long, and frequently occur early in the morning or around sun down.

## GEOGRAPHY

The US Virgin Islands are part of the Virgin Islands, a group of about 90 small islands and cays in the West Indies, starting about 40 miles (64km) from the eastern tip of Puerto Rico. They are just under 1,100 miles (1,771km) east of Miami, and about 1,500 miles (2,415km) south of New York.

The island chain is at the western end of the Lesser Antilles, extends for about 60 miles (96km) from east to west and lies in the Anegada Passage, the channel that connects the Atlantic Ocean and the Caribbean Sea. Generally, the Atlantic Ocean is to the north and the Caribbean to the south of the islands.

The Virgin Islands cover an area of about 195sq miles (507sq km) and are administered as two groups, the British Virgin Islands and the Virgin Islands of the United States. The British Virgin Islands, a former British colony, consist of four larger and 32 smaller islands covering 59sq miles (153sq km) and these lie to the north and east of the United States Islands.

The US Virgin Islands, under the administration of the US Department of the Interior as an unincorporated territory, consist of three larger islands —

# SUNSEEKER HOT SPOTS

**CHARLOTTE AMALIE – ST. THOMAS**
historic district, shopping
page 48

**CHRISTIANSTED – ST. CROIX**
historic district, shopping
page 101

**CORAL WORLD – ST. THOMAS**
page 74

**HISTORIC FREDERIKSTED**
wonderfully preserved old town, eateries, shopping
page 115

**HOTEL 1829 – ST. THOMAS**
best island dining
page 57

**MAGENS BEACH – ST. THOMAS**
page 76

**OFF THE WALL, CANE BAY – ST. CROIX**
unforgettable diving experience
page 112

**ST. GEORGE'S BOTANIC GARDEN – ST. CROIX**
page 120

**ST. JOHN NATIONAL PARK**
best walking
page 93

**TRUNK BAY – ST. JOHN**
page 87

St. Thomas, St. Croix and St. John — and about 50 smaller islets and cays, some no more than large rocks jutting out of the water, which together cover about 133sq miles (345sq km).

The islands are all peaks of submerged mountains, most of them extinct volcanoes, rising from a submarine plateau. The rocks are mostly sedimentary dating back about 100 million years. The waters around the islands are generally not more than 165ft (50m) deep, but they plummet to about 15,000ft (4,573m) in the trench which separates St. Croix from the other islands to the north. Note: This trench called the 'Puerto Rico Trench' lies north of St. Thomas. The Lesser Trench between St. Croix and St. Thomas, called the 'St. Croix Deep' is 2,580 fathoms. The three main islands are hilly with Crown Mountain on St. Thomas the highest point in the US Virgin Islands at 1,556ft (474m).

St. Croix is the largest island and is 28 miles (45km) long and covers an area of 82sq miles (213sq km). It is about 40 miles (64km) south of the two other main islands in the US Virgin Islands. St. Thomas covers an area of 32sq miles (83sq km) and St. John has an area of about 20sq miles (52sq km).

St. John is the most easterly of the US Virgin Islands and is only ½ mile (1km) to the west of Great Thatch Island in the British Virgin Islands.

St. Thomas consists of a range of hills and has little level land. Crown Mountain is north of the capital Charlotte Amalie, which sprawls over the hills that run down to the large natural and landlocked harbour. There are a few springs on the northern side of the island but only one small stream, and freshwater is always scarce. Magens bay in the centre of the north coast has more than 3,500ft (1,067m) of beautiful white sand beach and is one of the finest beaches in the Caribbean. St. Thomas is surrounded by many islands and cays, the largest of which are Water Island in the mouth of Charlotte Amalia Bay, and Hans Lollik Island off the mid-northern coast.

St. Croix is hilly in the north with Mount Eagle 1,088ft (332m) and Blue Mountain 1,165ft (355m), and the land slopes to plains and lagoons in the south. There are reefs along the north and south

*Preceding page: Sapphire Beach Resort, St Thomas*

coasts and few sheltered bays and inlets. There are some streams but fresh water is a scarce commodity. The eastern tip of St. Croix is the most easterly Atlantic point of the United States.

St. John is 3 miles (5km) east of St. Thomas across Pillsbury Sound, and has steep hills and valleys with little flat land. The highest peaks are Camelberg Peak 1,193ft (364m), and Bordeaux Mountain 1,277ft (389m), and the island has a forested, indented coastline with many sheltered bays and coves. Coral Bay, on the eastern end of the island, has a steeply sloping coastline which allows large vessels to anchor close to shore. The island has a number of springs and streams so water is less of a problem than on the other two islands.

More than three-quarters of St. John, including Hassel Island in St. Thomas harbour, is protected and preserved as the Virgin Islands National Park.

## HISTORY

The islands have had a turbulent history. They were frequently fought over by the great trading nations between the sixteenth and eighteenth centuries, pirates used them as bases, they were the scenes of slave uprisings and the slaughter of the Indian populations.

The early history of the islands is still being unravelled, and the first settlers are likely to have been Amerindians from South America who paddled their way northwards through the Caribbean in their dug out canoes, thousands of years ago. There is evidence of settlements around what is now Charlotte Amalie which date from 1500BC.

The peaceful Arawaks and other cultures from South America followed them dating from around 2,000 years ago, and the Tainos (Arawaks) were wiped out by the warlike Caribs, who migrated through the Antilles after AD1000. On St. Croix, Taino Indians from Puerto Rico established settlements but many were killed by the Caribs, although some were kept as slaves.

The original name of the Caribs was Kalina, meaning 'we alone are people'. The Spanish confused this with their word 'cariba', which was short for 'caribales' meaning cannibal, and this was shortened to carib. They were accomplished potters and weavers, and this was noted by Columbus when he visited the island on 14 November 1493 with

## BEACHES

All three island's boast superb white sandy beaches, and there is public right of access to all beaches. The best of the many fine beaches includes Magens Beach on St. Thomas, which was rated by National Geographic magazine, as 'one of the three most beautiful beaches in the world'. Check locally for any swimming safety risks.

Others include:

**St. Thomas** — Bolongo Beach, Brewers Bay, Coki Beach, Cowpet Bay, Hull Bay, Limetree Bay, Lindberg Beach, Morningstar Beach, Sapphire Beach, Secret Harbor, Stumpy Bay and Vessup.

**St. Croix** — Altona Lagoon, Buccaneer, Buck Island, Cane Bay, Cormorant Beach, Cramer Park, Davis Bay, Grapetree, Protestant Cay, Pelican Cove, Rainbow, Reef Beach, Sandy Point, Sprat Hall and Stoney Ground.

**St. John** — all the beaches are great, but especially Honeymoon Beach, Trunk Bay, Hawk's Nest, Caneel Bay, Cinnamon Bay, Maho Bay and Francis Bay.

## TANNING SAFELY

The sun is very strong but sea breezes often disguise just how hot it is. If you are not used to the sun, take it carefully for the first two or three days, use a good sun screen with a factor of 15 or higher, and do not sunbathe during the hottest parts of the day. Wear sunglasses and a sun hat. Sunglasses will protect you against the glare, especially strong on the beach, and sun hats will protect your head.

If you spend a lot of time swimming or scuba diving, take extra care, as you will burn even quicker because of the combination of salt water and sun. Calamine lotion and preparations containing aloe are both useful in combating sunburn.

Sea urchins, jelly fish and fire coral should all be avoided in the water.

*Facing page: Caneel Bay*

17 ships and 1,500 men under his command. His overall impression, however, was of a hostile population.

He anchored in what is now known as Salt River Bay on the north coast of the island and named the island Santa Cruz (Holy Cross). A landing party was sent ashore for fresh water and supplies following an attack on the Caribs but the Spanish, fearful of the Caribs' reputation as cannibals, fled and Columbus sailed away to explore the other islands nearby. He named that island chain Santa Ursula y las Once Mil Virgees (St. Ursula and the Eleven Thousand Virgins). It is said that as he sailed past, the islands spread out before him in the sea mist, reminded him of the painting depicting the British princess, St. Ursula and the 11,000 kneeling virgins who were massacred in Cologne by the Huns in the fourth century.

European explorers gave the islands a wide berth until 1512 when a large Spanish force landed, attacked the Caribs, and claimed the territory for the Holy Roman Emperor, Charles V (Charles I of Spain), although it was already Spanish by virtue of Columbus' discovery in 1493. For the next 40 years the Caribs were hunted down and many, it is claimed, were taken as slaves to work in the gold mines of Hispaniola — now the Dominican Republic and Haiti. By the end of the century, all had been killed, enslaved or had fled the islands.

The waters around the islands were frequented by English, French and Dutch pirates who preyed on the treasure-laden Spanish galleons. Sir Francis Drake who defeated the Spanish Armada in the English Channel, frequently sailed these waters as a privateer, and could have used St. Croix as his base.

The first major settlement in the Virgin Islands was by Dutch pirates who established a base on Tortola in 1648. In 1666 they were ousted by the Engish, and Tortola and the other islands to the east have been under British control ever since.

## ST. THOMAS

Small settlements wide apart had been established by a handful of English, Dutch and French in the 1620s and 1630s, but on 30 March 1666, a Danish force led by Erik Smidt landed on St. Thomas and claimed it for the Danish crown. The Danes did not have enough food to stay on the island for long and sent back urgent messages for provisions, but before these could arrive, a Dutch force under the command of Huntman landed and ousted the Danes. The Dutch were themselves evicted in 1672 when Jorgen Iverson landed at the head of an expedition from Copenhagen and funded by the Danish West India and Guinea Company. He became the island's Governor and established a farming settlement to supply Denmark with tobacco, cotton, indigo and other tropical crops. The island was divided into 177 plantations each of 125 acres (50 hectares), but the land was poor and hilly, and not suited to this sort of intensive farming. Nevertheless, 2 years later the first African slaves were transported to St. Thomas to work in the sugar cane plantations, and shipments of slaves were arriving regularly by 1681. The island's prosperity developed more because of the visiting merchant ships and slavers, than the plantations, and St. Thomas harbour became one of the busiest and most important in the West Indies. The galleons with their cargoes of treasure offered rich pickings for pirates and privateers, and many — Captain Kid, Blackbeard, and Bluebeard — chose to operate from St. Thomas. Many of the warehouses that still stand along the harbour waterfront, were filled with both legitimate merchants' goods, and booty captured by the pirates, while Market Square became one of the busiest slave markets in the Caribbean. The island's reputation was so bad, that British Admiral Benbow described St. Thomas as 'a recepticle for thieves'. In 1685 Denmark entered into a treaty with the Duchy of Brandenberg which allowed the duchy to establish the Brandenberg American Company, a slave trading post, on St. Thomas.

## ST. JOHN

Three years later, the Danes claimed St. John. They also had to oust the English from Tortola and the Leeward Islands, who regularly visited St. John to cut timber which they burned for charcoal. In 1717, several St. Thomas settlers moved to St. John to establish plantations but these were destroyed in 1733 after a bloody uprising by the slaves who held the island for 6 months. The proud African tribesmen thought it demeaning to work the land and were subjected to horrific punishments for refusing,

## SHOPPING

Shopping is a real treat on the islands. The free port status of St.Thomas means there is a huge range of merchandise at duty-free prices from the latest fashions, cameras and electronic gadgetry, to superb crystal, china, watches, jewellery and perfumes. You will find all the big names such as Cartier and Gucci, as well as fascinating island stores, galleries and boutiques where you can find local arts and crafts to buy as souvenirs, as well as paintings by local artists, and produce made from locally grown fruit and vegetables, and of course, the island rum. Tapes of island music also makes a permanent souvenir.

Shopping hours vary from island to island. Shops in the main tourist centers are usually open Monday to Saturday from 9am to 5pm, and often later. Shops will often open on Sunday if there is a cruise ship in port. Shops in rural areas and many of those on St. John follow the West Indian custom of closing for lunch. Many of the hotels and resorts have shopping arcades with longer opening hours, and the out of town shopping malls stay open later to cater for islanders wanting to shop after work. Always check to see if the shop accepts credit cards if you do not have much cash on you.

The main shopping area in St. Thomas is in and around Main Street in Charlotte Amalie, and do not forget to explore the surrounding alleys and passages down to the waterfront, with their interesting shops, boutiques and eateries. Also check out the Havensight Mall near the cruise ship terminal.

In St. Croix the best shopping is in the harbour area of Christiansted. Of special note is College Art Galleries on Company Street which exhibits work by local artists, and King's Ransom in King's Alley which offers local arts and crafts, and on St. John, the Wharfside Village has some interesting shops, and Mongoose Junction has several shops displaying work by local artists and craftsmen.

Best souvenirs include Caribbean and island jewellery, batik clothing, island herbs and spices, bay rum fragrances, local food products — such as jellies, pepper sauces and rum.

Works by local artists are exhibited and sold on Estate Tutu at the Tillett Gallery which is open Monday to Saturday 9am to 5pm.

*Old warehouses in Frederiksted, St Croix, now a new shopping development*

including amputations and floggings. In 1733 St. John was hit by hurricanes, supplies were scarce and many of the plantation owners simply starved their slaves. The new Governor of the islands introduced even more draconian measures, with most forms of disobedience punishable by torture and then death, and on the Sunday morning of 13 November 1733, the slaves rebelled. Fort Frederiksvaern was attacked first and all but one of the soldiers killed. The rest of the island was then taken and many white settlers were massacred, the plantations burned and the mills and great houses destroyed. For 6 months the slaves remained in control of the island. An attempt by a small British naval force to re-take the island failed, and it was not until a force of 400 French soldiers from Martinique had surrounded the slaves that the rebellion was finally over. The leaders, rather than surrender and face torture and death, either killed each other or jumped over the cliffs to their deaths in the sea.

## ST. CROIX

St. Croix has had the stormiest history. By 1642 the Dutch had established a settlement at what is now Christiansted, while the English were based at what is now Frederiksted. The two settlements were involved in many bloody disputes, and in 1645 the English murdered the Dutch Governor after the English Governor had been assassinated. The Dutch fled the island leaving it under the control of the English. In 1650 a Spanish expeditionary force of 1,200 soldiers from Puerto Rico landed and killed many English settlers. They also saw off a Dutch invasion attempt but had to surrender to a much larger French force led by De Poincy, Governor of the French West Indies, and left the island. The island was claimed for the French Crown and sold by the King in 1651 to De Poincy, a leading member of the Order of the Knights of Malta. The Order established a colony in 1653, divided the land into plantations and built fortifications and the townships. They also changed the island's name from Santa Cruz to its French translation of St. Croix. The colony, however, did not flourish, mostly because the Knights were soldiers not farmers, and in 1665 they sold it to the French West India Company. It reverted back to the French crown in 1674, the year after the first African slaves were introduced to work in the sugar cane plantations.

In 1695, however, the French King had decided that there was not much future for St. Croix, and he ordered all the inhabitants to pack up and move to the plantations on St. Domingue. For almost the next 40 years, the island languished, and its future looked bleak.

In 1733 the Danish West India and Guinea Company bought St. Croix from the French King for 750,000 'Livres' ('pounds'), and by 1742 had imported more than 1,900 slaves to work the plantations. The island's prosperity boomed for a time, but the Danish East India and Guinea Company policy gradually caused economic stagnation, and the islanders petitioned the Danish King for relief. In 1754 St. Croix was officially declared the property of the Danish Crown.

From 1755 the Danish Crown established an administrative capital at Christiansted, St. Croix and Charlotte Amalie was declared a free port. All the islands flourished, and for almost 50 years were considered neutral territory by the great powers. St. Croix and St. John produced sugar cane and distilled rum, and St. Thomas and its free port remained a major trade and slave center, and continued to be used by pirates and privateers because of its neutrality which afforded them protection.

Despite their alleged official neutrality, the Danish sided with the American colonists against the British in their fight for independence, and in 1776 the Danes became the first foreign power to salute the flag of the newly declared United States of America, when a salvo was fired from the cannon of Fort Frederik in St. Croix.

The British seized the islands in 1801 after Denmark had sided with France in the Napoleonic Wars and in 1803, after they were returned to Denmark, slave trading was abolished throughout the Danish West Indies, although the ownership of slaves was still permitted by Denmark. The islands were again seized by the British in 1807 and they remained in occupation until 1815 when they were returned to Denmark.

During this period there were a number of fires in Charlotte Amalie which largely destroyed the town causing it to be completely rebuilt.

The islands remained under Danish control until 1917, and

during this period law and order was established. The pirates were kicked out, and the last buccaneer was hanged in St. Thomas in 1825.

In 1847 the Danish crown announced that slavery was finally to be abolished, but there was a sting in the tail. In order to alleviate the effect on the plantations, slavery was to be phased out over the next 12 years. It caused considerable unrest on the island forcing Governor von Scholten, in defiance of the Crown, to immediately free all the slaves. The end of cheap labour saw a steady decline in the plantations' prosperity and many closed. The situation for the jobless islanders became so desperate that led by 'Queen Mary', among others, the laborers rebelled in 1878. The rebellion was quickly dealt with, but recognising their plight, the Danes formally tried Queen Mary, later freeing her.

The St. Thomas islands then became the refuge for many political exiles, including Santa Anna, the Mexican General who defeated the Texans at the Alamo.

In 1867 the Danes offered to sell the islands to the United States, but a move by the US Senate to buy them in 1870 for $7.5 million was defeated. In 1917, however, during World War I, the US purchased all three islands for $25 million from the Danish Government because of their strategic importance on the main passage through the Caribbean to the Panama Canal. There were fears that the Germans might buy the islands and use them as naval bases to attack shipping in the area.

The islands became an unincorporated territory of the US although the Danish administrative structure was retained to ensure a smooth take over. In 1917 there were just 4 miles (6km) of roads on St. Thomas and no education available beyond elementary (primary) school. In 1927 an act was passed granting US citizenship to the islanders. From 1917 to 1931 the island was administered by the US Navy Department with a Governor appointed by the US President, until March 1931, when jurisdiction was transferred to the Department of the Interior and Paul Person, the first civilian

*Facing page: One of St Croix's many fine beaches*

Governor was sworn in.

The Organic Act, passed in 1936, gave the islanders a limited franchise and established two municipal councils, one for St. Thomas and St. John, and the other for St. Croix, under a territorial council. In 1954 under the Revised Organic Act, the councils were scrapped and a central Government system was introduced. However, it was not until 1970 that the islanders elected their first Governor and legislature by popular franchise, and not until 1972 that they were able to send a delegate, Ron de Lugo, to the House of Representatives.

## WEATHER

The weather on the US. Virgin Islands is undoubtedly one of its greatest attractions. The sun almost always shines but there is usually the gentle cooling breeze of the trade winds from the ocean which helps reduce humidity. Temperatures rarely rise above 90°F (32°C), or fall below 70°F (21°C). The average temperature is about 77°F (25°C), during the winter months, and 82°F (28°C) during the summer.

Rainfall averages between 45 and 50 inches a year (114 and 127cm) although this varies enormously from year to year. Most days each month are rain free. Some parts of the islands which are in rain shadows, have less than 30 inches (76cm) a year, while the higher mountain slopes can receive more than 80 inches (203cm). The dry season lasts from January to June and the wet season from July to December with September, October and November the wettest months, although even then it often only rains for 5 or 6 days on average each month. Water is in such short supply that all buildings have their own systems for capturing as much as possible, although most rain water still runs away.

Drinking water supplies are still shipped in by barge when necessary, but several desalination plants operate on St. Croix and St. Thomas and the islanders have become very adept at using sea water whenever possible.

The area is in the hurricane belt and managed to avoid almost all the major storms in the area over the past 100 years until 1989, when St. Croix was hit by Hurricane Hugo which caused widespread damage and left most of the islanders homeless. Miraculously, most of the historic buildings received little damage.

Statistically, only four hurricanes hit the island every 100 years, and before 1989 the previous hurricane hit in 1932. The hurricane season lasts from July to October, although tropical storms and hurricanes can occur in June and November, and are most likely in August and September. Please note that in September 1995 parts of the US Virgin Islands were devastated by Hurricane Marilyn The area is also geologically active and minor submarine earthquakes do occur occasionally.

## THE PEOPLE

The population is split between St. Thomas and St. Croix, both of which have a population of around 55,750 and St. John which has a population of about 3,500. The people of St. Thomas are known as St. Thomians (pronounced Tow-mians), those from St. Croix as Crucians (pronouned Crew-shuns), and those from St. John as Johnians (pronounced Jo-nians). St. Thomas and St. Croix are very much West Indian islands, although St. Croix is similar in many ways to mainland US with its farming, manufacturing and population, many of whom are 'continentals' — that is from mainland US not Europe, and St. John is the most natural and least developed.

The vast majority of the population is descended from African slaves, although there is an increasing minority from other Caribbean islands, including Puerto Rico. More than half the population, however, are immigrants to the islands.

The Cachas of St. Thomas are a distinct ethnic group, descended from French Catholics, who moved to the island at the end of the nineteenth century from Saint Barthélémy when it was sold by Sweden to the French in 1877. They maintain their own customs and traditions and are mostly engaged in fishing and farming.

The official language is English although most of the islanders speak a lilting patois known as Calypso, which varies slightly from island to island. While the various forms are understood by the islanders, Calypso is generally incomprehensible to visitors. Some French is spoken on St. Thomas, and Spanish is spoken on St. Croix where there is a sizeable population from Puerto Rico.

Most islanders are Catholic although there is a large minority of Anglicans and many other religious denominations are represented. The Lutheran Church in Charlotte Amalie is the second oldest in the Western Hemisphere and held its first

*The harbour at Christiansted, St Croix*

service in 1666, while the second oldest American synagogue is on St. Thomas.

## CULTURE

The islands do not have their own specific culture and heritage as such, because the population is so mixed and many people are relatively recent immigrants. The strong mix of cultures, however, reflect the island's varied colonial past and there is a strong tradition of music, song and dance, as there is throughout the Caribbean. In 1965 the Virgin Islands Council of the Arts was established and community arts councils have been founded on all three islands to sponsor cultural events and promote arts and crafts. There are regular performances by local and international artists at the Reichhold Center for the Arts in St. Thomas on the campus of the College of the Virgin Islands, and at the Pistarkle Theater at Frenchman's Reef. On St. Croix a wide variety of cultural events are staged at the Island Center, and on St. John, there are programmes of music at Cruz Bay. Many hotels also feature local singers, bands and dance groups.

St. Croix and St.Thomas both have ballet groups which blend classical and modern dance with traditional folk. The Quadrille is still a traditional dance of the islands, although it has been adapted from the version originally brought by the Europeans. On St. Croix they dance the Imperial Quadrille, which was performed in the courts of Europe in the eighteenth century, and some of the calls are still given in French. On St. Thomas, they dance the Flat German Quadrille which starts out as very stately with a waltz step, and then moves on to the Calypso step and finally the 'Flirtation'.

St. John hosts an annual Festival of the Arts with free events at Maho Bay and Cruz Bay, and the St. Croix Jazz and Caribbean Music and Arts Festival extends over 11 days in October. The US. Virgin Islands Folklore Festival is held every 3 years on St. Croix in association with the Smithsonian Institution.

There are several galleries exhibiting the work of local artists, mostly on St. Thomas and these include Riise's Gallery, Camille Pissarro Gallery in the Camille Pissarro Building, Jonna White Gallery in Palm Passage which can all be found in Charlotte Amalie, Frederick Gallery in Havensight, and Mango Tango Gallery at Al Cohens Plaza. There are 'Arts Alive' festivals three times a year at Estate Tutu.

Charles Hawes, 'the Dean of St. Croix Art' lives in Frederiksted, and is one of the island's most famous artists, a member of the American Watercolor Society and a Life member of the Society of Illustrators. Born in 1909, he has worked for the *Chicago Tribune, Life and Look*, and moved to St. Croix in 1965 where he specialises in painting island scenes.

There are a number of special festivals, notably the St. Croix Christmas Fiesta and the St. Thomas Carnival. The former starts on Christmas Day and lasts for 12 days until Epiphany, which is celebrated as the Feast of the Three Kings and concludes with a huge costumed parade through Christiansted. This Crucian festival was celebrated during Danish rule and became formalised before World War I. The festival is really the island's Carnival, and although it officially lasts one week, celebrations usually start ahead of Christmas and last beyond Epiphany.

Carnival on St. Thomas takes place shortly after Easter, unlike many other islands where it precedes this Christian festival, but in every other respect it is a full-blown week-long West Indian Carnival with fantastic costumes parades (Saturday), Mocko Jumbi stilt walkers, steel band and calypso competitions, beauty pageants, and lots of singing, dancing and merrymaking. Highlights include the Coronation of the Queen of Carnival, the King of the Band, the Children's Parade (Friday) and the J'Ouvert Morning Tramp — an early morning steel band parade which wakes everyone up. The Mocko Jumbi are an important part of carnival. The brightly dressed 'spirits', usually with mirrors sown into their costumes, strut around on their 17ft (5m) high stilts. Mocko Jumbi, means 'make believe spirit', and legend has it that they were invisible. The idea of the mirrors is that when you look at the Mocko Jumbi all you can see is a reflection of yourself. Many of the events take place in Carnival Village and most evenings there are jump-ups or street parties with lots of singing, dancing and feasting. Carnival is a good time to see many of the traditional dances brought from Africa, which were themselves based on centuries-old rituals. The St. Thomas Carnival is now regarded as one of the most spectacular in the West Indies. St. John holds its annual carnival during the first week of July.

## ECONOMY

Tourism is the island's main income earner, and there are few other economic resources. Some sand and gravel is excavated for local construction needs, and light industries include rum distillation, textile and pharmaceutical manufacture and watch factories. The exception is the oil refinery on St. Croix, one of the largest in the world, which was built in 1966 and produces petroleum products, the island's main export. Crude oil is the main import, followed by food, and the Government is by far the largest employer, employing almost one third of the entire labour force, mostly in administrative jobs. Attempts are being made, however, to reduce this top-heavy bureaucracy and to transfer many services from the public to the private sector.

Tourism reached around 1.8

million in 1988, the year before Hurricane Hugo, and more than 60 per cent of these visitors landed from cruise ships. Today, the islands regularly receive almost 2 million visitors annually, again more than half from cruise ships.

The island group retains its own taxes and receives financial assistance from the United States, and as a result has one of the highest per capita incomes in the Caribbean, which accounts for the influx in recent years of people from other Caribbean islands seeking employent and higher living conditions. It has to be added that the islanders also have to pay much higher prices, while wages remain traditionally low. The influx of 'continentals' from the US mainland, has also driven up the cost of land and this is another area of continuing friction.

In the past, the islands' economy was based on sugar cane and cotton. Fishing for export has never been commercially significant, although there is a sizeable fleet supplying local needs and fish is an important part of the diet. Game fishing is becoming increasingly important as an income generating industry. Charlotte Amalie is a free port.

## ADMINISTRATION

The islands come under the jurisdiction of the US Department of the Interior. There is adult suffrage and a one chamber legislature of 15 Senators, each elected for 2 years by popular vote. The Governor and Lieutenant-Governor are also elected. Administration is divided into three branches — executive, legislative and judicial — controlled by 12 departments, 11 headed by a Commissioner and the Law Department under the control of the Attorney General. The US Virgin Islands are represented in the US House of Representatives by a non-voting delegate. Islanders are not eligible to vote in the US Presidential elections. There have been frequent attempts to approve a constitution for the Virgin Islands, all so far unsuccessful.

There are municipal courts and a Federal District Court, education is compulsory and free, although there are a large number of private schools, and the University of the Virgin Islands was established in 1962, and has campuses on St. Thomas and St. Croix. There is a well developed health service with a general hospital on St. Thomas and permanent facilities on St. Croix and St. John. Mobile health units regularly visit the other smaller islands.

## FLORA & FAUNA

The islands have a wide variety of habitats, consisting mostly of lush tropical vegetation although the soil layer is not deep, except on St. John. The main vegetation zones consist of tropical coastline with mangrove swamps, tropical rain forest, mountain and near-desert belts. There are wonderful flowering plants and trees such as jasmine, orchids, hibiscus, poinsettia, thryallis and bougainvillea, the amazing century plant, which blooms every 10 years or so, and the delicate yellow ginger thomas, the national flower. Although hibiscus and bougainvillea bloom everywhere, neither are native to the islands. Bougainvillea, named after a French explorer, was brought to the West Indies from Brazil in the early 1700s, while the hibiscus comes from Hawaii. The flamboyant tree with its spectacular red flowers originally came from Madagascar, while the African tulip tree comes from West Africa. The frangipani, however, is a native of the islands, and one of the most spectacular flowering trees.

The soil is not generally rich enough and the rainfall not heavy enough to produce good stands of commercial timber, although mahogany trees were imported towards the end of the eighteenth century, and there is West Indian ebony. There are many species of palm and other common species include boxwood, red-barked turpentine, strangler fig, bay rum, sandbox, fiddlewood, kapok, yellow cedar, maho, wattle, cinnamon and buttonwood.

Many of the trees are grown for their fruit. These include fig, mango, guava, sugar apple, soursop, coconut and breadfruit. The seagrape, which can be found along many beaches, produces edible fruit, but is much more important because its roots prevent sand erosion.

Cacti and acacia abound in the lowland areas, while many species of orchid can be found in the hills. A survey of the St. Croix identified more than 40 species of orchids. The lowland areas are generally used to grow sugar cane. On St. John, more than 300 species of plants have been recorded and more than 200 species of birds, both resident

*Facing page: A Kapok tree with big buttress roots*

and migratory.

The islands have a rich wildlife both on land and in the sea. St. John boasts 800 species of trees, shrubs and plants. The woods support a number of animals, including small deer, and there are more than 1,000 species of marine life.

The marine wildlife is even more spectacular. There are scores of species of brightly-coloured fish to be seen in and around the coral reefs, while the warm waters teem with larger fish, especially game fish such as tarpon, tuna, barracuda, jacks, sailfish, marlin, kingfish, swordfish and wahoo. There are also queen conch, southern stingray, long-spined black sea urchin, and green, hawksbill and saddleback turtles, all threatened species. Coral is very delicate and should not be touched and never damaged or removed. Some coral, such as fire coral, needs treating with great caution, but most are beautifully coloured and safe, and are meant to be enjoyed. The most common corals include seafan, staghorn, elkhorn, brain, large star, pillar and orange reef.

Coral reefs are the ocean's equivalent to tropical rain forests, and only grow in waters with a year-round temperature of 68°F (20°C). Stony coral grows less than a ½ inch (1.25cm) a year, and staghorn, the fastest growing coral in the eastern Caribbean, only grows between 4 and 6 inches (10 and 15cm) a year.

Whale watching is a popular pastime from February to April as humpback whales pass by the islands on their annual migration, and there are many boat trips to see them.

Island wildlife includes bats, both fruit and fish-eating, small numbers of white tailed deer in the St. Croix hills, and the mongoose, which was said to have been imported from Asia to kill rats that flourished in the sugar cane plantations. The largest animals to be seen are the Senepol cattle found on St. Croix, a cross breed between the traditional English Red Poll and the drought-tolerant Senegal from Africa. There are several species of lizards including iguana and gecko, and anoles which are able to change their colour like chameleons. Islanders consider the iguana a delicacy, but it is now protected. Insects can be a nuisance, especially mosquitoes, and there are large numbers of wasps and termites, especially on St. Croix. Tarantulas may make you shudder but they are relatively harmless, as are scorpions which are extremely rare.

The black and yellow sugar bird, or banana quit, is the islands' territorial bird, and the 'yellow bird' in the famous calypso of the same name. Other species include hummingbirds, parrots, parakeets, and the black parrot-like ani, egrets kingbirds, doves, thrushes, sparrows, crows and several types of bird of prey. Around the coast and out to sea, you can spot brown pelicans, the magnificent frigate bird, great blue heron, white-tailed tropicbird, gulls and terns.

As most of the plants, fruits, vegetables and spices will be new to the first time visitor, the following brief descriptions are offered:

**Bananas** are one of the Caribbean's most important exports, thus their nickname 'green gold' — and they grow everywhere. There are three types of banana plant; the bananas that we normally buy in supermarkets originated in Malaya and were introduced into the Caribbean in the early sixteenth century by the Spanish. The large bananas, or plantains, originally came from southern India, and are largely used in cooking. They are often fried and served as an accompaniment to fish and meat. The third variety is the red banana, which is not grown commercially, but which can occasionally be seen around the island. A banana produces a crop about every 9 months, and each cluster of flowers grows into a hand of bananas. A bunch can contain up to 20 hands of bananas, with each hand having up to 20 individual fruit.

Although they grow tall, bananas are not trees but herbacious plants which die back each year. Once the plant has produced fruit, a shoot from the ground is cultivated to take its place, and the old plant dies. Bananas need a lot of attention, and island farmers will tell you that there are not enough hours in a day to do everything that needs to be done. The crop needs fertilising regularly, leaves need cutting back, and you will often see the fruit inside blue tinted plastic bags, which protect it from insect and bird attack, the sun's rays and speed up maturation.

The **Bay tree** is a native of the Windward Islands, a member of the Laurel family and can grow to a height of 30ft (9m). The leaves can be crushed for their oil which is used in the perfume industry. The leaves are used in cooking.

**Breadfruit** was introduced to the Caribbean by Captain Bligh in

## A NOTE OF
## WARNING
### THE MANCHINEEL

The manchineel, which can be found on many beaches, has a number of effective defensive mechanisms which can prove very painful. Trees vary from a few feet to more than 30ft (9m) in height, and have widely spreading, deep forked boughs with small, dark green leaves and yellow stems, and fruit like small, green apples. If you examine the leaves carefully without touching them, you will notice a small pin-head sized raised dot at the junction of leaf and leaf stalk. The apple-like fruit is poisonous, and sap from the tree causes very painful blisters, and was used as a poison. It is so toxic, that early Caribs are said to have dipped their arrow heads in it before hunting trips, and an effective, and apparently often used untraceable method of killing someone in olden times, was to add a few drops of the sap to their food over a period. The sap is released if a leaf or branch is broken, and more so after rain. Avoid contact with the tree, do not sit under it, or on a fallen branch, and do not eat the fruit. If you do get sap on your skin, run into the sea and wash it off as quickly as possible.

1793. He brought 1,200 breadfruit saplings from Tahiti aboard the *Providence*, and these were first planted in Jamaica and St. Vincent, and then quickly spread throughout the islands. It was Bligh's attempts to bring in young breadfruit trees that led to the mutiny on the *Bounty* 4 years earlier. Bligh was given the command of the 215-ton *Bounty* in 1787 and was ordered to take the breadfruit trees from Tahiti to the West Indies where they were to be used to provide cheap food for the slaves. The ship had collected its cargo and had reached Tonga when the crew, under Fletcher Christian, mutinied. The crew claimed that Bligh's regime was too tyranical, and he and eighteen members of the crew who stayed loyal to him, were cast adrift in an open boat.

*A ruined sugar mill at Annaberg, showing the old windmill*

The cargo of breadfruit was dumped overboard. Bligh, in a remarkable feat of seamanship, navigated the boat for 3,600 miles (5,796km) until making landfall on Timor in the East Indies. Some authorities have claimed that it was the breadfruit tree cargo that sparked the mutiny, as each morning the hundreds of trees in their heavy containers had to be carried on deck, and then carried down into the hold at nightfall. It might have proved just too much for the already overworked crew.

Whatever the reason for the mutiny, the breadfruit is a cheap carbohydrate-rich food, although pretty tasteless when boiled. It is best eaten fried, baked or roasted over charcoal. The slaves did not like it at first, but the tree spread and can now be found almost everywhere. It has large dark, green leaves, and the large green fruits can weigh 10 to12lbs (4 to 5kgm). The falling fruits explode with a loud bang and splatter the pulpy contents over a large distance. It is said that no one goes hungry when the breadfruit is in season.

**Calabash trees** are native to the Caribbean and have huge gourd like fruits which are very versatile when dried and cleaned. They can be used as water containers and bowls, bailers for boats, and as lanterns. Juice from the pulp is boiled into a concentrated syrup and used to treat coughs and colds, and the fruit is said to have many other medicinal uses.

**Cinnamon** comes from bark of an evergreen tree, also related to the laurel. The bark is rolled into 'sticks' and dried, and then ground or sold in small pieces. It is used as a spice, for flavouring, and adds a sweet, aromatic flavour to many dishes. Oil from the bark is used to flavour sweets, soaps, toothpastes and liqueurs, while oil from the leaves is used in perfumes.

**Cocoa** is another important crop, and its Latin name *theobroma* means 'food of the gods'. A cocoa tree can produce several thousand flowers a year, but only a fraction of these will develop into seed bearing pods. It is the heavy orange pods that hang from the cocoa tree which contain the beans which contain the seeds that produce cocoa and chocolate. The beans, containing a sweet, white sap that protects the seeds, are split open and kept in trays to ferment. This process takes up to 8 days and the seeds must be kept at a regular temperature to ensure the right flavour and aroma develops. The seeds are then dried. In the old days people used to walk barefoot over the beans to polish them to enhance their appearance. Today, the beans are crushed to extract cocoa butter, and the remaining powder is cocoa. Real chocolate is produced by mixing cocoa powder, cocoa butter and sugar.

You can buy cocoa balls or rolls, like fat choclate fingers, in the markets and village shops, which make a delicious drink. Each ball is the size of a large cherry. Simply dissolve the ball in a pan of boiling water, allow to simmer and then add salt, sugar and milk or cream, for a rich chocolate drink. Each ball will make about four mugs of chocolate.

**Coconut palms** are everywhere and should be treated with caution. Anyone who has heard the *whoosh* of a descending coconut and leapt to safety, knows how scary the sound is. Very few people do get injured by falling cocounts and that is a near miracle in view of the tens of thousands of palms all over the island. However it is not a good idea to picnic in a coconut grove!

Coconut trees are incredibly hardy, able to grow in sand and even when regularly washed by salty sea water. They can also survive long periods without rain. Their huge leaves, up to 20ft (6m) long in mature trees, drop down during dry spells so a smaller surface area is exposed to the sun which reduces evaporation. Coconut palms can grow up to 80ft (24m) tall, and produce up to 100 seeds a year. The seeds are the second largest in the plant kingdom, and these fall when ripe.

The coconut traditionally bought in greengrocers, is the seed with its layer of coconut surrounded by a hard shell. This shell is then surrounded by a layer of copra, a fibrous material, and this is covered by a large green husk. The seed and protective coverings can weigh 30lb (13kgm) and more. The seed and casing is waterproof, drought proof and able to float, and this explains why coconut palms which originated in the Pacific and Indian Oceans, are now found throughout the Caribbean — the seeds literally floated across the seas.

The coconut palm is extremely versatile. The leaves can be used as thatch for roofing, or cut into strips and woven into mat and baskets, while the husks yield coir, a fibre resistant to salt water and ideal for ropes and brushes and brooms. Green coconuts contain a delicious thirst-quenching 'milk', and the coconut 'meat' can be eaten raw, or baked in ovens for 2 days before being sent to processing plants where the oil is extracted. Coconut oil is used in cooking, soaps, synthetic rubber and even in hydraulic brake fluid.

As you drive around the island, you will see groups of men and women splitting the coconuts in half with machetes preparing them for the ovens. You might also see halved coconut shells spaced out on the corrugated tin roofs of some homes. These are being dried before being sold to the copra processing plants.

**Dasheen** is one of the crops known as 'ground provisions' in the eastern Caribbean, the others being potatoes, yams, eddo and tannia. The last two are close relatives of dasheen, and all are members of the aroid family, some of the world's oldest cultivated crops. Dasheen with its 'elephant ear' leaves, and eddo

*Trunk Bay*

grow from a corm which when boiled thoroughly can be used like potato, and the young leaves of either can be used to make callaloo, a spinach-like soup. On the US. Virgin Islands, however, this soup is traditionally made from spinach and kale, and it is spelt 'kallaloo'. Both dasheen and eddo are thought to have come from China or Japan but tannia is native to the Caribbean, and its roots can be boiled, baked or fried. Callaloo is still grown in gardens and can be seen growing wild.

**Guava** is common throughout the islands, and the aromatic, pulpy fruit is also a favourite with birds who then distribute its seeds. The fruit bearing shrub can be seen on roadsides and in gardens, and it is used to make a wide range of products from jelly to 'cheese', a paste made by mixing the fruit with sugar. The fruit which range from a golf ball to a tennis ball in size, is a rich source of vitamin A and contains lots more vitamin C than citrus fruit.

**Mango** can be delicious if somewhat messy to eat. It originally came from India but is now grown throughout the Caribbean and found wherever there are people. Young mangoes can be stringy and unappetising, but ripe fruit from mature trees which grow up to 50ft (15m) and more, are usually delicious, and can be eaten raw or cooked. The juice is a great reviver in the morning, and the fruit is often used to make jams and other preserves. The wood of the mango is often used by boatbuilders.

**Nutmeg** trees originally came from the Banda Islands in Indonesia and for centuries its source was kept secret because it was such a valuable commodity to the merchants selling it. In 1770 a French naturalist raided the islands, then under Dutch control, and stole several hundred plants and seedlings which were planted on Mauritius and in French Guyana, but these almost all died. At the end of the eighteenth century Britain was at war with Napoleon Bonaparte and Holland, which had allied with France. The British captured the Banda Islands during the war and before they handed them back in 1802 as part of the Treaty of Amiens, they had learnt the secret of the nutmeg and successfully planted it in Penang in Malaya, and tropical territories around the world, including the West Indies. The tree thrives in hilly, wet areas and the fruit is the size of a small tomato. The outer husk, or pericarp, which splits open while still on the tree, is used to make the very popular nutmeg jelly, delicious when spread on toast, desserts or meat.

Inside, the seed is protected by a bright red casing which when dried and crushed, produces the spice mace. Finally, the dark outer shell of the seed is broken open to reveal the nutmeg which is dried and then ground into a powder, or sold whole so that it can be grated to add flavour to dishes.

In Victorian times it was fashionable to carry a nutmeg or wear it in a pendant to ward off illness, and the islanders still use grated nutmeg to help fight colds.

**Passion fruit** is not widely grown but it can usually be bought at the market. The pulpy fruit contains hundreds of tiny seeds, and many people prefer to press the fruit and drink the juice. It is also commonly used in fruit salads, sherbets and ice creams.

**Pawpaw trees** are also found throughout the islands and are commonly grown in gardens. The trees are prolific fruit producers but grow so quickly that the fruit soon becomes difficult to gather. The large, juicy melon-like fruits are eaten fresh, pulped for juice or used locally to make jams, preserves and ice cream. They are rich sources of vitamin A and C. The leaves and fruit contain an enzyme which tenderises meat, and tough joints cooked wrapped in pawpaw leaves or covered in slices of fruit, usually taste like much more expensive cuts. The same enzyme, papain, is also used in chewing gum, cosmetics, the tanning industry and, somehow, in making wool shrink-resistant. A tea made from unripe fruit is said to be good for lowering high blood pressure.

**Pigeon peas** are widely cultivated and can be found in many back gardens. The plants are very hardy and drought resistant, and give prolific yields of peas which can be eaten fresh or dried and used in soups and stews.

**Pimento**, or allspice, was introduced from Jamaica. The dried berries are said to have the combined flavours of cinnamon, clove and nutmeg, which is how it gets its name. The dried fruit is used for pickling, for curing meat and flavouring wines, and it is usually an ingredient in curry powder. An oil extracted from the berry and leaf is used in the perfume and pharmaceutical industries.

**Pineapples** were certainly grown in the Caribbean by the time Columbus arrived, and were probably brought from South

America by the Amerindians. The fruit is slightly smaller than the Pacific pineapple, but the flavour more intense.

**Sugar apple** is a member of the annona fruit family, and grows wild and in gardens throughout the islands. The small, soft sugar apple fruit can be peeled off in strips when ripe, and is like eating thick apple sauce. It can be eaten fresh or used to make sherbet or drinks.

**Soursop**, is a member of the same family, and its spiny fruits can be seen in hedgerows and gardens. It is eaten fresh or used for preserves, drinks and ice cream.

**Sugar cane** is no longer grown commercially on any of the islands and molasses is imported for the rum distilleries. Cane can still be seen growing, however, in the wild and in some gardens. The canes can grow up to 12ft (4m) tall and after cutting, the canes have to be crushed to extract the sugary juice. Most estates had their own sugar mill powered by water wheels or windmills. The remains of many of these mills can still be seen around the islands, as well as much of the original machinery, mostly made in Britain. After extraction, the juice had to be boiled until the sugar crystalised. The mixture remaining was molasses and this is used to produce rum.

**Turmeric** comes from the dried root and underground stems of a plant, which is a relative of ginger. The bright yellow spice is used to flavour foods and as a colouring. It is also used as a dye.

The **Vanilla plant** is a climbing member of the orchid family which produces long, dangling pods containing beans. The vanilla is extracted by distilling the beans and is used as a food flavouring, as well as in the pharmaceutical industry.

## FOOD & DRINK
### Food

You can dine in style on the islands enjoying international cuisines from around the world, or the best of Creole cooking. You can experiment with local vegetables and enjoy the freshest of fish and shellfish, or sample the many ethnic restaurants, from Mexican to Chinese and Tex-Mex to finest French. There is also a wide range of fast food outlets for those who want to eat in a hurry and get back out into the sun as quickly as possible. Remember, however, that this is still the Caribbean and there is not the

*Alamandas and Hibiscus compliment good food to round off the day at the Sapphire Beach Resort*

same degree of urgency experienced elsewhere, so if you think things are taking a long time, order another drink, relax and take in the view.

St. Thomas has the most restaurants and the greatest choice, but there is both elegant and relaxed dining to be found on St. Croix where there is a mix of both hotel restaurants and privately run establishments. On St. John the dining is more informal, with the emphasis often on the freshest ingredients presented simply for the fullest

*Facing page: Cinnamon Bay, St John*

flavours. On all three islands, however, one of the great attractions is being able to dine alfresco.

Most hotels and large restaurants accept credit cards but to avoid embarrassment always check first to make sure that if you do need cash you have enough.

It seems a shame, however, to visit the islands and not enjoy their excellent local dishes. There is wonderfully fresh seafood, especially lobster, conch (pronounced conk), yellowfin tuna, grouper and wahoo, a large mackerel type fish. Crabcakes are a speciality of the islands, as are conch fritters.

Try Caribbean black bean soup, conch chowder or kallaloo, a rich soup made from spinach and kale with pieces of pepper, flakes of fish, crab and meat and often, spiced up with pepper. Kallaloo, can sometimes be spelt calaloo or callaloo. Bullfoot soup is another meal in itself, made with meat and vegetables with local spices and seasonings.

Do not be confused by 'fungi' on the menu. These are steamed dumplings made from okra and cornmeal, and commonly served as a side dish. Other vegetables often served include fried plantain and pigeon peas, and rice is usually served rather than potatoes.

Souse is another island speciality, a delicious meat stew in which lots of unmentionable bits from the pig are used, including head and tail. Curries were brought to the islands by Indian labourers in the mid-nineteenth century, and are delicious. They can feature conch, chicken, lamb or mutton (goat).

There are wonderful fresh fruit juices, and the fruit is also used to make tasty desserts which often include soursop ice cream or sapodilla pudding.

Eating on the move or out of doors can also be very enjoyable, and there are many opportunities to eat from the snack bars on the street or by the beach. This 'street food' ranges from juices and ice creams flavoured with local fruits, to hot snacks such as fritters, patties and roti. Most of this food is fried but it is usually wholesome, delicious and cheap. Snacks include pork chops, conch fritters, fried pumpkin slices, and johnny cakes (unleavened fried bread). Patties and pates, are pastry envelopes filled with seafood or spiced meat, especially beef, and rotis, which originated in the East Indies, are another form of soft pastry envelope stuffed with curried meats or vegetables. Take care if ordering a chicken roti, because in many places the meat contains small bones, which some people like to chew on!

## *Drink*

The first West Indian rum was produced in the Danish Virgin Islands around 1674 and by the end of the century, there were more than 275 distilleries on the islands. Rum became an important commodity and figured prominently in the infamous Triangle Trade in which slaves from Africa were sold for rum from the West Indies which was sold to raise money to buy more slaves.

Rum had such fortifying powers that General George Washington insisted every soldier be given a daily tot, and a daily ration also became a tradition in the British Royal Navy. There are still a number of distilleries on the islands producing rum using traditional methods, and most can be visited and their wares tasted and purchased. All sorts of rums are produced on the island from light to dark and of varying strengths, but Virgin Island rum has traditionally been noted and sought after for its lightness, balance and dryness.

Rum features in many of the island's most popular cocktails, but there are many excellent local soft drinks as well, such as mauby, sometimes maubi, made from a mixture of herbs, bark and ginger, or sorrel, made from the flowers of the plant.

There are also many different sorts of herbal and fruit teas available which make great thirst quenchers and revivers.

### Planter's Punch

Combine 2 ounces each of pineapple juice, rum, cream of coconut and half an ounce of lime in a blender for one minute. Pour into a chilled glass, add a sprinkle of coconut shavings and garnish with a cherry and a slice of orange.

### Rum Punch

Mix one part lime or lemon juice, two parts of sugar syrup (equal quantities of sugar and water brought to the boil and then allowed to cool before using), three parts of rum and four parts of water. Pour over crushed ice and add a slice of orange or a wedge of pineapple.

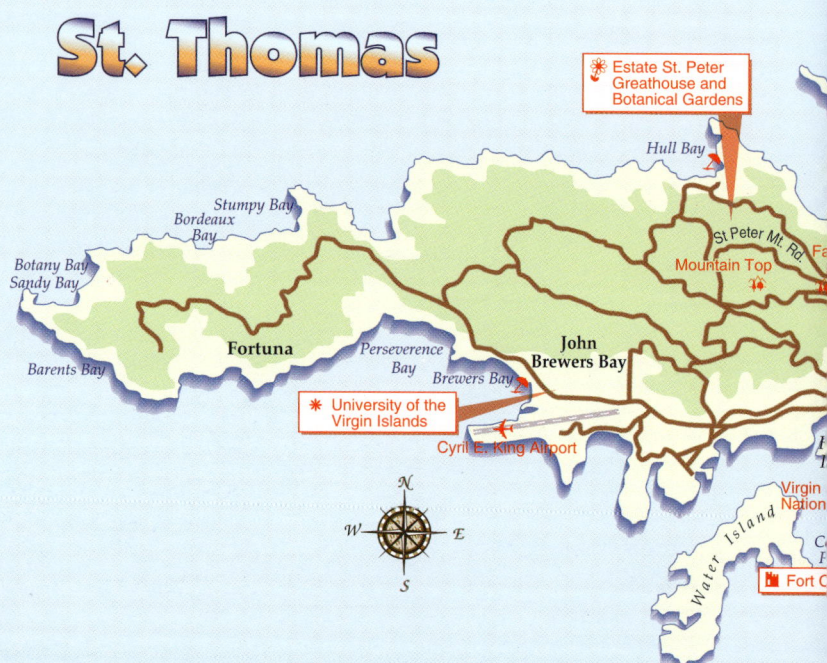

# Touring & Exploring the U.S. Virgin Islands

The islands have a reasonably good road network, although conditions vary enormously, and all are small enough to be explored comfortably on foot if you want to. Taxis, mini-buses and hire cars are available on all three islands and there are reasonably regular passenger bus services on St. Croix and St. Thomas. There are regular boat services between St. Thomas and St. John with several sailings each way every day. The crossing takes 20 minutes and costs $3 each

way. Ferries run at 6.30am, 7.30am and 8am and then hourly until midnight. There are also several sailings Monday to Saturday between Charlotte Amalie and Cruz Bay. The 45-minute crossing costs $7 each way. Ferries from Charlotte Amalie run from 9am-7pm, and from Cruz Bay between 7.15am and 5.15pm.

Larger vessels, both seagoing passenger and cargo ships, call at Charlotte Amalie on St. Thomas and Frederikstad and Limetree Bay on St. Croix, but there are no ferries between St. Thomas and St. Croix. There is also a ferry service between Charlotte Amalie on St. Thomas and Tortola in the British Virgin Islands. If you plan on taking the ferry for a day trip to Tortola, remember to carry your passport. The crossing takes about an hour including custom formalities.

A high speed ferry, the *Fast Cat*, started operating at the end of 1995, offering a 70-minute service between Christiansted, St. Croix, and Charlotte Amalie, St. Thomas. There are several sailings daily and the one way fare for adults is $25, and $15 for children.

There are also regular flights between St. Thomas and St. Croix. You can also fly between the islands by Virgin Island Seaplane Shuttle (☎ 773-1776), or take a helicopter if you really want to travel quickly, or to be dropped off at a secluded beach for an idyllic picnic, before being picked up again. The seaplane terminals are on the waterfront at Charlotte Amalie on St. Thomas, at Christiansted on St. Croix and Cruz Bay on St. John, and Antilles Helicopters are based at Frenchman's Reef (☎ 776-7880).

# ST. THOMAS

The island faces the Atlantic Ocean to the north and the Caribbean Sea to the south and a ridge of mountains run east to west through the center of the island. The mountains do slow travel down and although distances between places on the island are not great, journeys often take longer than planned. It is the second largest of the US Virgin islands, the most accessible and the most densely populated. The Cyril E. King International Airport is on the south coast west of Charlotte Amalie.

## CHARLOTTE AMALIE

St. Thomas's fortune has been built on its vast natural, deep water harbour which plays host to about 1,000 cruise ships and thousands of yachts every year, and is overlooked by the delightful and historic capital of Charlotte Amalie. In the harbour, privateers like Sir Francis Drake and pirates like Captain Kidd anchored their vessels between harrying the Spanish treasure ships, and it was also used by notorious pirates such as Bluebeard and Captain Kidd. Today, it is one of the most popular ports of calls in the Caribbean for cruise ships. The town was officially established in 1681 when Governor Esmit ordered the building of 4 taverns to the west of the fort. At that time there were only 39 inhabitants living in a single row of houses along the north side of what is now Main Street. By 1716, there were 82 houses and several large warehouses, and by 1789 the town's population had grown to 2,082. By 1801, there were more than 1,000 buildings and 3,500 residents. In 1804 a fire swept through the town destroying 1,200 houses and other buildings, but rebuilding was swift.

Today, the bustling city has scores of old buildings, most more than a hundred years old and many much older which survived the frequent fires that swept through the city between 1804 and 1837. In 1825 the town was hit three times by disaster, the first two being hurricanes, and then a fire which destroyed more than 1,000 buildings.

A census conducted in 1837 found there were 140 different nationalities on the island, and Charlotte Amalie was the third largest city in the Danish Kingdom. The many old buildings reflect the architectural styles of several nations, particularly French, Spanish, Dutch, Danish and now, modern American. There is the elaborate French ironwork, typical of many Creole buildings, traditional Dutch doors, and airy tiled Spanish patios which provide shelter from the sun during the hottest parts of the day. There are narrow, cobbled streets and alleys, and these too reflect the island's colourful Colonial past, with English, Danish and French names. On Main Street (Dronningen's Gade), buildings were numbered as they were built which explains the lack of any logical order, and many of the streets have several names to add to the confusion.

The capital, named in 1730 after the consort of Christian V, was originally called Tap Hus, which roughly translated meant 'rum or grog shop', and then Amalienbord. The city's red roofed white and pastel-coloured buildings sprawl in a series of terraces over the three hills now named Denmark, Synagogue and Government, and many parts have changed little over the past 200 years. The hills used to be known as Fioretop, Main and Mizzen by the sailors of the sailing ships who moored in the harbour.

The multi-coloured houses hug the hillsides, amid lush vegetation and flowers that seem to bloom year-round, and there are magnificent private mansions and hotels higher on the hills.

During the day the city bustles with shoppers, traffic and tourists and at night there are many nightspots to enjoy.

The only way to see the city is on foot and most of the interesting and historic sights are contained within a few downtown blocks. A walking tour is essential as many of the places to be visted are down narrow picturesque alleys, and it is important to stop frequently and look up to take in the fine ornamentation on many of the upper storeys of buildings. The

## GETTING AROUND ST THOMAS

Hire a car for total freedom to explore the island, but if you only plan to go on occasional trips, take taxis or travel by public bus, one of the easiest ways of really getting to know the islanders. There are scores of trips and excursions to take, and you can explore the island on one of the open safari buses, by foot and even on horseback.

Taxis do not have meters and while some regularly used fares are fixed — by destination not mileage, such as from the airport to various hotels — others are a matter of negotiation. Always agree on a price before setting off. The following are typical charges from the airport to Charlotte Amalie $4.50, from Charlotte Amalie to Bolongo Bay $7, Coral World $7.50, Magens Bay $6.50, and to Red Hook $9. There are extra charges for luggage (50c for each large item) and a $1.50 late night surcharge. All taxis have licence plates which begin with the letters 'TP'.

An easy way to save money is to share a taxi, so ask around to see if anyone else is going your way, and do not be surprised if your taxi suddenly brakes en route to let someone else on board, either another fare or just a friend. Taxi drivers are usually very knowledgable and make excellent guides, and they always know just the right place to stop for lunch. You can hire taxis by the hour or day for extended tours, but always agree beforehand how much you are going to be charged.

Open safari buses leave Market Square for Red Hook every hour from 8.15am to 5.15pm, and from Red Hook to Market Square every hour from 7.15am to 5.15pm. The one way fare costs $2. There are also Manassah buses which run between Charlotta Amalie and Red Hook between 6am and 8pm. They are cheaper but there is no official schedule and while they come along at roughly 20 minute intervals, they are often packed.

waterfront area makes a good place to start the walking tour which takes in most of the historic buildings as well as the excellent shopping.

Start by visiting the striking red **Fort Christian**, built in 1672 and completed in 1678. The clock tower was added in 1784. It was one of the five forts built by the Danes on the islands. Its location in town is slightly unusual but when it was built more than 300 years ago on the waterfront, there were few other buildings and it commanded a very strategic position protecting the harbour. In times of the trouble, the entire population was able to shelter within its walls. Over the years it has been added to, and used for various purposes. It was first a fort, then a Lutheran church, court, Governor's Residence, police station and prison, and it is now a National Historic Site and houses the Virgin Islands Museum with fascinating displays of natural history and Arawak and Carib artifacts, as well as Post-Columbian exhibits. There are also a number of large baskets which were used by the women to carry coal, a reminder of the days when coal fired ships arrived in port to take on board more fuel. In the courtyard there is an old animal drawn mill, and a small bay rum still. There are great views over the town and harbour from among the cannon on the battlements.

Over the years a number of infamous pirates were tried and executed in the fort. The red bricks used to build the fort were brought across the Atlantic as ballast in the ships which returned to Europe carrying sugar cane, rum and cotton. The fort museum, which includes the dungeons, is open from 8.30am to 4.30pm Monday to Friday, from 9.30am to 4.30pm on Saturday, and from 12noon to 4.30pm on Sunday. Admission is free.

Across Veterans Drive and between the fort and the waterfront, is the lime-green Italian-Renaissance-style **Legislature Building**, originally built in 1874 as a barracks for Danish troops. It was here that the ownership of the islands was officially transferred from Denmark to the United States in 1917, and it was later used as a high school, and then barracks for US Marines, before becoming the Legislature in 1957. There is a pretty garden in front of the Legislature's impressive stepped main entrance, and from it, there are great views across the harbour. The Senate Chambers are open to the public between 8am and 5pm Monday to Friday.

Cross over Veterans Drive again to visit the **Vendors Plaza**. Everything from local arts and crafts to fabrics and fashions are sold from the stalls sheltered from the sun under a canopy of multi-coloured umbrellas. Things to look out for include handmade jewellery, belts, island costume dolls, straw goods and hand-painted ornaments.

Just inland from the Vendors Plaza is **Emancipation Park** which is a delightful place to spend some quiet time and enjoy the shade and floral displays, especially when the lignum vitae trees are in bloom. The park commemorates the abolition of slavery in the Danish West Indies on 3 July 1848. It is a popular meeting place, especially on special occasions and public holidays. There is a gazebo which is used for occasional band concerts, a bust of King Christian IX, and a replica of the US Liberty Bell. The area around the park is also a useful place to pick up a taxi as most people coming in by cab are dropped closeby.

Cross over Tolbode Gade for the **Tourist Office** in the cream coloured building on the corner. There is a hospitality lounge where you can get your bearings, get some relief from the sun and find out what is going on around the island. There are also rest rooms. Just up the road is the Old Danish Customs House, now a crystal and china shop, and on the corner is the yellow-painted **Post Office**. The building is officially known as Emancipation Garden Station and in the lobby are two fine murals painted by *Evening Post* illustrator Stevan Dohanos in 1941, and depicting the waterfront and fort. Opposite are three statues honouring Virgin Island educators.

From the corner of Tolbod Gade look across at the imposing façade of the **Grand Hotel** with its upper storey pillared-porticos, which stands north of Emancipation Gardens. The massive building, built in Greek Revival-style in 1840, was originally the Commercial Hotel and Coffee House. A hurricane removed the top floor at the end of the nineteenth century, so now there are just two. The building houses shops and offices.

Walk along Norre Gade with the Grand Hotel on your right. On the left there is the yellow-painted **Bethania Hall**, which serves as the parish meeting rooms. It was orginally a Danish manor house built at the beginning of the nineteenth century, and later the home of Jacob H.S. Lind. It has also been a post office, school and home for the elderly.

Next door and up the steps, is the beautiful Gothic revival-style

*Following pages: Sapphire Beach*

**Frederick Lutheran Church**, the third church on this North Street site. It was built in 1793, replacing churches built in 1750 and 1789. The present building was gutted by fire in 1826 and damaged by hurricane in 1870. The church congregation dates back to the 1660s when the first Danish settlers arrived, making it the second oldest Lutheran Congregation in the New World. It has a fine collection of ecclesiastical silver, which is still used on special occasions, many interesting plaques and a quaint old chandelier. Also on Norre Gade is the Moravian Church built between 1882 and 1888. Moravian churches are found on all the US Virgin Islands. The Moravians came from Czechoslovakia and were a reformist sect several decades before Luther, and as such they suffered great persecution in Europe.

Across the junction on the corner of Norre Gade and Fort Strade is the elaborate grey **Old Cable Building** built in Queen Anne-style complete with cupola at the end of the nineteenth century.

Head inland, and then climb the steps to Kongens Gade (King's Street). The area around Government Hill has a number of old and historic buildings including Government House, Blackbeard's Castle, Hotel 1829, Crown House and the Street of 99 Steps.

The imposing three-storey neo-Classical **Government House** which stands overlooking a small park with a fountain on Government Hill, was built in the late 1860s to replace an 1819 building, and is the office and official residence of the Governor. The first two floors are open during the week for tours, and they have many treasures, including works by Pissarro and many other fine local artists. It has its original wooden floors and a fine two-storey high wrought iron balcony. In the lobby there are a number of murals painted in the 1930s by Pepino Mangravatti depicting historic scenes — the arrival of Columbus, the 1917 transfer of the the islands to the US and a working sugar plantation. He came back in 1974 to sign them. The house is open weekdays between 8am and 12noon and 1 and 5pm. Admission is free.

To the right is **Seven Arches Museum**, a fully restored eighteenth century Danish artisan's residence. It has a separate Danish kitchen and the house with period furnishings, overlooks Charlotte Amalie. Tours are conducted by the owner between 9am and 3pm Tuesday to Sunday. There is a small admission charge. After visiting the museum, you can take a drink in the walled garden. Next but one from the museum is the white Lieutenant Governor's Office.

On the other side (west) of Government House separated by the steep stone steps, is the **Frederik Lutheran Church Parsonage** built around 1725 and still serving that purpose today.

Continue along Kongens Gade with the waterfront on your left to the **Street of 99 Steps**, said to have been designed by planners who never visited the island and had no idea how steep the terrain was. The road builders went ahead anyway and used the plans to build the street which connects Government Hill with Little Tower Street to the north and they had to incorporate all the 'steps' to make it safe. Take your time and walk up the steps counting them as you go if you have the puff, and then ask yourself why the street has this name (there are actually 103 steps)! The various coloured bricks used in the construction came in as ballast aboard ships — mostly red from England and yellow from Denmark.

Turn right at the top of the steps and follow the road round and up past the old yellow brick Anglican parsonage built in the 1700s, to **Blackbeard's Castle** on Blackbeard's Hill. The castle, now a hotel, is named after the infamous English pirate Edward Teach from Bristol, and the tower was built in 1679, amid the ruins of Fort Syktsborg. The round tower is 31ft (9m) high and its walls are 5ft (1½m) thick at the base, and it was one of several defensive look-outs built around the town to alert the fort of attacks from the sea. Blackbeard is reputed to have lived there at the end of the eighteenth century and was killed by the British in hand to hand fighting off North Carolina in 1718. The tower is the oldest structure in the Virgin Islands.

Return down the '99' steps and turn right into Kongens Gade to visit **Hotel 1829**, once the magnificent home of a French sea merchant named Lavalette, and now a charming hotel with a lovely courtyard and fine dining. It has been restored to maintain its original town house atmosphere and preserve the natural wood and stone craftsmanship. It gets its name from the year it was built. The initials of the original owner can still be seen in the balcony's wrought iron grillwork.

Hotel 1829 has a superb restaurant with fabulous food, an exceptional wine list and thoroughly professional, attentive service. The list of after-dinner drinks is larger and better than most other hotel's entire wine lists. If you like cigars, the selection has to be one of the largest in the Caribbean outside Cuba. Fine dining always

comes at a price, but this is worth every penny.

The westernmost house on Government Hill is the 1854 Hus, a former private residence now housing a restaurant, offices and shops.

At the top of the steps leading down to Garden Street, look across at the mini-White House complete with flags on the hill opposite. This is Catherineberg built in 1830 and until 1993, the official residence of the President of the West Indian Company, the company that owned the Havensight Cruise Ship docks until they were sold back to the US. They are now owned by the Government.

Turn right into Garden Street and then cross over into Crystal Gade. On the south-eastern corner with Nye Gade is **St. Thomas Reformed Church** built in 1846 in Greek Revival-style with its massive façade columns. Further along on the opposite side is the Gothic **St. Thomas Sephardic Synagogue** (full name Beracha Veshalom Vegimulth Hasidim, meaning Blessing, Peace and Loving Deeds). The congregation was formed in 1796 and is the second oldest in the Western Hemisphere. The present building on Raadet's Gade, dates from 1833 after the first two temples were both destroyed by fire, the second time after a massive blaze which ravaged the city in 1831. The Jewish community on the island was established about 1781with Sephardic Jews escaping Spanish persecution, and emigres from the Dutch island of St. Eustatius, which had been attacked by Admiral Rodney during the American Revolution. The Dutch island had been supplying the Americans and so Rodney's ships bombarded the island destroying many of the homes, including the Jewish quarter and the synagogue. In 1824 there were 64 Jewish families on St. Thomas and in 1684, Gabriel Milan, the first Jewish Governor was appointed by the Danish King Christian V. Another prominent Jew, Benjamin Franks, led the fight to oust pirates from the island, and he was a main witness in the trial of Captain Kidd in 1701. Other famous members of the Congregation include author Herman Wouk, Governor Ralph Paiewonsky and eminent island historian Isidor Paiewonsky. The synagogue floor is traditionally covered with a sprinkling of sand to commemorate the Exodus of the Jews from Egypt. It is also said the sand was used to muffle the sounds of their worship when

*Facing page: Bluebeard's Castle, Charlotte Amalie*

Judaism was banned.

Cut back a short way along Crystal Gade and then head south past Back Street into **Main Street**. The main shopping area is along Main Street, also called Dronningen's Gade, in the centuries-old terracotta warehouses built by Danish merchants. The materials used to build many of the warehouses, including Spanish marble and Italian tiles, reflects the wealth of the island's merchants. Over the years the warehouses have stored sugar, rum, cotton and even human cargoes, and many have been restored to their former glory, and now retail a wide range of luxury items from jewellery, perfumes, silver, china and crystal. Even if you do not wish to buy, it is worth visiting the shops to view the warehouses with their massive arches, elaborate brickwork, stone floors and thick walls. One of these shopping areas is called the Beretta Center, in honour of one of the men who had the idea of scraping away decades of grime from the walls of the buildings to reveal their hidden beauty.

On Main Street at number 14, through the black wrought iron gates, is the **Camille Pissarro Building** where the French impressionist painter Camille Pisarro was born and spent his childhood, although the plaque commemorating this is in Back Street (Vimmelskaft's Gade) which has a number of charming little shops and eateries. In the courtyard, there is a sign outlining the artist's life on the island and his subsequent fame in Paris. The artist's parents are buried in the Jewish Cemetery in St. Thomas, and two of his works are displayed in Government House.

Running off Main Street to the harbour are a number of delightful narrow alleys, some of which still have the iron rail tracks on which freight was pushed on wagons between the ships and the warehouses. They have intriguing names such as Drake's Passage, Riise's Alley and Palm Passage, and are filled with small but interesting shops, boutiques and eateries.

Continue west along Main Street and you come to Rothschild Francis Market Square. Just before the square on the right is the pink **Enid M. Baa Library**. It was built in the mid-1850s as a private home and was one of the first buildings erected in compliance with the newly-introduced regulations designed to reduce the risk of fire.

In the seventeenth and eighteenth centuries, the **Market** was one of the busiest slave markets in the Caribbean. It is estimated that up to 250,000 slaves were sold through the market before being shipped off to plantations in the United States and other Caribbean islands. It was known as Casimir Square in the 1800s in honour of the father of Governor von Scholten. He was responsible for introducing new building regulations to reduce the risk of devastating fires. These banned wood roofs in favour of tile and slate, and introduced wide streets and courtyards to prevent flames spreading. The covered market, known as The Bungalow, was built at the beginning of the twentieth century. Its iron roof is believed to have come from a European railroad company. Local produce is sold every day except Sunday, and Saturday is busiest. It is a good place to see the wide range of exotic spices, fruits and vegetables grown on the island. Try the genips — a very refreshing small fruit which you tear open and eat the flesh from around the stone.

From the Market you can take Strand Gade down to the Waterfront and then turn left and follow the Caribbean back to Emancipation Park and the taxis.

If you are feeling fit you can continue past the fort to visit the cruise ship dock and surrounding shopping area. Cruise ships land their passengers at the West India Company dock which is at the eastern end of the harbour in the area known as Homeport. If planning a visit to Charlotte Amalie, it is always a good idea to check how many cruise ships are visiting that day, because that determines how busy the city will be and how congested the roads around it. If there are a lot of cruise ships arriving in port, it may be prudent to put off your visit to the capital until a quieter day. There is a good duty free shopping complex opposite the dock in the Havensight Mall, and you can visit the Bay Rum Factory at the Caribbean Market Place. The factory produces the famous bay rum fragrances for which the island is noted.

## OTHER THINGS TO SEE AND DO FOR SHORT OUTINGS

**Fort Cowell** is at **Cowell Point** on **Hassel Island** which stands in the mouth of St. Thomas harbor. There has been a small fort on the point for more than 200 years and it is now named after Colonel Cowell, the British officer who accepted the surrender of St. Thomas from the French during the Napoleonic Wars on 1 April 1801. Under his

*Following pages: Charlotte Amalie harbour*

command the fort was further strengthened. **Signal Hill** on the island has been used as a look-out point for centuries. The island was part of the mainland until the 1860s, when the navy cut through the narrow peninsula separating it with a narrow channel. The land was owned by the Paiewonsky Brothers, and they sold it to the Department of the Interior so that it could become a National Park.

The **Danish Consulate** is on Denmark Hill and was built in 1830 in a mix of Classical and Greek Revival styles, and close by is Villa Santana which dates from 1858. Crown House was the official residence of the Danish Governor and was built in 1750. It has many fine features including domed ceilings and original furnishings, including a hand carved four poster bed. The stone house was once the official home of Governor Peter van Scholten, and although now privately owned, it is open Monday to Saturday between 10am and 5pm.

The **Atlantis Submarine** operates daily from close to the West India Company Dock. The 48-seat observation submarine dives to about 15 fathoms (90ft) to allow passengers a close-up view of marine life around the reefs of Buck Island National Park. The submarine offers day and night dives. ☎ 776-0288. Reservations are recommended during peak periods.

To the east and easily seen atop the hill is **Bluebeard's Castle**, now a hotel with fine views over the harbour. It stands at the top of Frederiksberg overlooking the harbour, and the tower is the oldest structure on the island. It was originally built in 1689 as Frederiksfort and was used as a fort until 1735. Legend has it that the notorious pirate Bluebeard lived in the tower when ashore, and that it is now haunted by him and some of his victims who met terrible deaths, although there is no evidence to support this. Certainly pirates like Bluebeard were welcomed by the island's Governors who believed it was better to have them as friends than as enemies. The original tower now stands in the gardens of the resort hotel, and its suites are very popular with honeymoon couples.

The restored Nisky Moravian Mission, dating from the late 1770s is on the Harwood Highway to the west of town, and close by is the Orchidarium which offers conducted tours.

Take the **Paradise Point Tramway**, a cable car which will take you 700ft (213m) above Charlotte Amalie for stunning views. It operates daily. ☎ 774-9809. There is a restaurant at the top and a number of boutiques.

## EATING OUT IN AND AROUND CHARLOTTE AMALIE

| Inexpensive | $ |
| Moderate | $$ |
| Expensive | $$$ |

**Cafe Amici** $$ Riise's Alley, Italian and Continental ☎ 774-3719

**Cafe Sigapo** $$ Government Hill, Mediterranean ☎ 776-0444

**Cafe Sito** $$ Waterfront, Spanish and seafood ☎ 774-9574

**China Garden** $-$$ Norre Gade, Cantonese ☎ 776-3256

**Cuzzins** $$ Back Street, Very popular restaurant offering seafood and tradional West Indian dishes ☎ 777-4711.

**Diamond Barrel** $-$$ Main Street, Creole specialities ☎ 774-5071. Great for lunch and dinner.

**Entre Nous** $$-$$$ Bluebeard's Castle, International ☎ 776-4050. Dinner only.

**Fiddle Leaf** $$$ Government Hill, Good modern cooking with the best of Creole and many other cuisines. ☎ 775-2810

**Glady's Cafe** $$ Main Street, West Indian ☎ 774-6604.

**The Greenhouse** $$ International Plaza, American-Mexican ☎ 774-7998. Open from breakfast to dinner.

**Hard Rock Cafe** $$ International Plaza, Burgers and American ☎ 777-5555.

**Hotel 1829** $$-$$$ Government Hill, Gourmet dining ☎ 774-1829.

**Lemon Grass Cafe** $-$$ Back Street, American-International ☎ 777-1877

**Little Bo Peep** $ Back Street, Creole ☎ 774-1959. The name is a pun on the name of owner Augustus Beaupierre. Great seafood. Open breakfast to dinner.

**On The Bay** $-$$ Windwood Passage Hotel, Waterfront, Caribbean ☎ 774-5200

**Palm Passage Cafe** $$ Palm Passage, Italian ☎ 774-2708.

**Petite Pump Room** $$ Upper Waterfront, West Indian ☎ 776-2976

**Sparky's Saloon** $-$$ Waterfront, Seafood and snacks ☎ 774-8015. The bar is a great place to try the

local drinks.

**Tasha's** $-$$  Gamle Gade, Creole
☎ 774-5826

**Taste of Italy** $$  Back Street, Italian
☎ 775-1090

**Tickles Dockside Pub** $-$$ Crown Bay Marina, American
☎ 776-1595

**Virgilio's** $$-$$$ Dronningen's Gade, Italian at its best
☎ 776-4920

**Williams and Daniels** $-$$
**Scandinavian Centre, Main Street,** French and Continental
☎ 776-8877

**Zorba's** $$  Government Hill, Greek
☎ 776-0444

## TOURING THE WESTERN HALF OF THE ISLAND

The tour leaves Charlotte Amalie by taking coast road route 30 — Veterans' Drive — west to **French Town** or 'Cha Cha Town', a community at the western outskirts of the capital. It was originally settled in 1848 by French emigres from the island of St. Barthelemy who were themselves descended from French Huguenots who had fled France to escape persecution from the Catholic authorities. Most came originally from fishing villages in Brittany and Normandy. They established a farm near Gallows Hill, and the settlement grew as more French immigrants arrived. The area now has a very distinct character of its own with French street names beginning with 'rue', and many popular restaurants and nightspots. The Roman Catholic Church of St. Anne stands on the small rise which overlooks French Town. The town gets its nickname because the early French immigrants, with their unusual clothes, were laughed at by the islanders. In retaliation, the French would shout 'cha cha', which loosely translated meant 'go to the Devil'. The name has stuck and the 'Frenchies' today still celebrate Bastille Day and the Feast Day of St. Anne, the patron saint of Brittany.

Continue east on route 30 where there is a turn off (route 304) to Sub Base, and continue past the international Cyril E. King Airport. To the north is the campus of the St. Thomas department of the College of the Virgin Islands, and the **Reichhold Center for the Performing Arts**. Tours of the center are given on days when there are no scheduled

*Preceding pages: Cruise ship and seaplane at Charlotte Amalie*

performances. The center has a wonderful outdoor theater which is used to stage a wide range of cultural events from classical music to jazz, and ballet to folk dance.

The college was founded in 1963 to meet the needs of both the Virgin Islands and neighbouring Caribbean Islands. Students attend a 4 year course for their Bachelor of Arts and Masters' degrees. The 175 acre (70 hectare) campus includes the Nursing Education and Science Buildings, lecture halls and dormitories.

The road now becomes **Brewers Bay Road** and runs past **Brewers Bay** whose beach is quite lively as it is popular with students from the college. It faces west and is a great place to watch stunning sunsets.

Beyond Brewers Bay, the road forks. The left hand fork continues west as Fortuna Road past **Perseverence** and **Fortuna Bays** where it ends by the sea. To the west, and reached either by car along a very rough road or on foot, is **Barents Bay** with **Sandy Bay** and **Botany Bay** side by side on the westernmost flank of the island. On the northern coast of this westernmost promontory are **Bordeaux Bay** and **Stumpy Bay**.

If you take the right hand fork at the junction, you are on West End Road which runs north and connects with the Crown Mountain Road which offers access to the feeder roads to the northern coastline.

Detour to the coast on the road to **Hull Bay** (route 303 then 404) where the beach is lined with trees which offer shade. There is a snack bar and good snorkelling around Longshore Reef. Many of the fishing boats to be seen along this stretch of coastline are owned by 'Frenchies', whose ancestors fled to St. Thomas more than 200 years ago from the French West Indies. They are a tight knit community and they speak in a slightly different way from other islanders. Hull Bay is popular with surfers because of its powerful Atlantic waves, but only strong swimmers should venture out to sea.

From Hull Bay, return to Crown Mountain Road and then drive east past **St. Peters' Mount**, at 1,500ft (457m), the island's tallest peak.

**Estate St. Peter Greathouse and Botanical Gardens** are off Estate St. Peter Road, reached by turning off Crown Mountain Road at the Four Corners Intersection. The 3 acres (1 hectare) of gardens, built on three levels, are set amid the volcanic peaks of St. Thomas, and packed with more than 500 species of trees and plants and stunning scenery and views. The Great House has displays of local artists' work. There is a self-guiding trail through the gardens and from the observation tower 1,000ft (305m) above sea level, there are fabulous views on most days over 20 surrounding islands. The gardens are open daily.

Pop in for a meal and drink, non-alcoholic if you are driving, at **Mountain Top**, which not only has incredible views, but offers some wonderful cocktails. The bar is reputed to be where the banana daiquiri was created. The observation area has spectacular views and there are a number of shops inside the main building.

**Fairchild Park** was a gift to the islanders from philanthropist Arthur Fairchild, and also offers tremendous panoramic views. It is open daily from dawn to dusk and is popular as a wedding location because of the views across Charlotte Amalie and the harbour. If you are looking for spiritual peace and quiet, visit the Little Chapel of Our Lady of Perpetual Help.

The route then returns south through the mountains back to Charlotte Amalie.

## EATING OUT ON THE WEST OF THE ISLAND

| | |
|---|---|
| Inexpensive | $ |
| Moderate | $$ |
| Expensive | $$$ |

**Alexander's Cafe** $-$$
Frenchtown, Austro-Italian
☎ 776-4211

**Barbary Coast** $$ Frenchtown, Lobster specialities and seafood
☎ 774-8354

**Bites of Paradise** $$-$$$
Frydenhos, true Caribbean
☎ 775-4747

**Cafe Normandie** $$-$$$
Frenchtown, Continental
☎ 774-1622

**Chester Chicken** $-$$ Çontant, West Indian ☎ 774-7470.

**Chez Jacques** $$-$$$ Frenchtown, from bistro to haute cuisine
☎ 776-5797

**Craig and Sally's** $$ Frenchtown, International ☎ 777-9949.

**Ferrari's Ristorante** $$ Crown Mountain Road, Italian
☎ 774-6800

**Hook, Line and Sinker** $-$$
Frenchtown, Seafood specialities with burgers, pastas and steaks
☎ 776-9708

**L'Escargot** $-$$ Sub Base, Creole, French and American
☎ 774-6565

**The Old Mill** $$ Contant, Italian
☎ 776-3004

*Above: The Grand Palazzo Hotel complex at Great Bay*
*Below: Great Bay*

**Provence Bistro** $$ Frenchtown, French ☎ 777-5600

**Sugar Reef Cafe** $-$$ Crown Bay, Excellent American and Continental ☎ 776-4466

**Johnny Cakes** $$ Frenchtown, Nouvelle Creole ☎ 776-2466.

**Victor's Hide Out** $$ Crown Bay, Creole and seafood ☎ 776-9379

## TOURING THE EASTERN HALF OF THE ISLAND

Take route 30 out of Charlotte Amalie which follows the waterfront past Bluebeard's Castle up on the hills on your left, and out past the West India Company dock where the cruise ship passengers disembark.

Route 30, like many of the roads on the island has many names, and as it leaves town, it becomes Frenchman Bay Road. The road is narrow and twisting in places but as it follows the Caribbean coast eastwards, there are fabulous views, and lots of opportunities to turn off for the descent down to the beaches. There are a number of hotels and resorts along this stretch of coastline, such as Frenchman's Reef Hotel, and neighbouring Morningstar Beach Resort. **Morningstar Bay** offers good snorkelling and there are lots of opportunities to pursue a wide range of watersports.

The road then changes its name again and becomes Bovoni Road past Limetree Beach, and then becomes Bolongo Road, as it runs past the fine **Bolongo Beach** where you can stop for a swim or a game of tennis at the Bolongo Beach Club. Buck Island stands off Bolongo Beach.

The road then runs past a small mangrove swamp where the trees with their incredible buttress roots stand in the water, to the Clinton Phipps Racetrack at Nadir, where races are held from time to time.

Route 30 then connects with route 32 and its name changes to Redhook Road, as it skirts round the eastern tip of the island, past Benner Bay, East End Lagoon and **Compass Point**, a favourite anchorage for visiting yachts which mingle with the local fishing boats. Just inland from Compass Point there is a wildlife preserve created by the local Rotary Club.

To the south lies the island of **Frenchman's Cap**. The US. Virgin Islands have many world-class diving sites and one of the finest is off this small island which lies about 1 mile (2km) south of the eastern tip of St. Thomas. The cove on the western side of the island is good for dives up to 40ft (12m), but the really spectacular dive is off the eastern coast where a submarine mountain falls steeply away, allowing wall dives down to 90ft (27m) in good weather conditions. The waters even at this depth, are remarkably clear, and you can swim among turtles, inquisitive groupers, and large rays. During February and March an added bonus may be the presence of gentle giant humpback whales on passage with their calves.

Back on the mainland route 322 branches east of route 32 for Secret Harbor Bay and Cowpet Bay. **Secret Harbor Bay** is usually quiet and offers excellent snorkelling. Equipment can be rented locally and there are a number of boats that will take you out to dive sites. There is another reef in the mouth of **Cowpet Bay** which has a fine beach fringed with trees which offer shade during the hottest part of the day.

North of Cowpet Bay is **Great Bay** and its northern promontory is the most easterly point on the island. Great Bay is dominated by the remarkable Grand Palazzo, a replica of a Venetian Palace, which opened in 1992 as a luxury resort, set in 15 stunning acres (6 hectares) of tropical gardens running down to the beach. Accommodation is in six buildings, each named after an island flower, which nestle in the hills. The hotel has generators and reverse osmosis and desalination machines, to provide all its own electricity and water needs. You can enjoy traditional afternoon tea and spectacular views

There are several other small but good beaches at **Nazareth Bay** and further along the coast. The area has become popular as a tourist area and a number of condominiums have been built along this stretch of coast. You can also visit the St. Thomas Yacht Club.

Redhook Road continues northwards, past the turn off for the Virgin Island **headquarters of the US National Park Service**, where there is a wealth of information about the islands, their wildlife, walks to do, and outdoor activities to take part in. The headquarters has its own dock at the southern end of Vessup Bay and at the northern end, reached by route 32, is the ferry for the 20 minute crossing to St. John. The island hop makes a great day out, but there is so much to see on St. John that you should really plan to spend longer if possible.

**Redhook Harbor** is in the middle of the bay and is the base for a number of charter boats offering sailing, diving and fishing trips, as well as mini-cruises to neighbouring islands.

To the east across the Pillsbury Sound there are usually excellent views of St. John.

Route 32 continues north to the

Atlantic Coast where it becomes route 38 — Smith Bay Road — and then it heads west past Sapphire Bay, Pelican Cove and Smith Bay. **Sapphire Bay** is perfectly named and the warm, clear waters are a delight to swim in, but care is needed as the area is also popular with windsurfers. Offshore the largest island, slightly to the west is **Thatch Cay**, with a chain of several small islands to its right. These are from left to right Grass, Mingo, Lovango and Congo Cays.

There is a botanical garden at the **Stouffer Renaissance Grand Beach Resort** which overlooks Winter Bay. There are guided tours at 10am on Fridays, and self-guiding tours can be undertaken at other times using the informative leaflet.

The next stop is **Coki Point**, home of **Coral World**, one of the island's main attractions. It is the perfect place for those who can't dive or snorkel but want to experience the wonders of the undersea world. Coral World, which covers 5 acres (2 hectares) is an undersea observatory built on three levels about 100 yards (92m) from the shore and extending 20ft (6m) below the surface. At each level you can watch at close hand life at different levels of the reef. Each morning at 10am, 11am and 2pm, you can also watch divers hand-feeding sharks, barracuda and other large fish in the reef tank. The aquarium has 21 tanks, each depicting marine life at different points around the Virgin Islands, as well as a marine garden, predator tank and touch tank. The park also boasts an 80,000 gallon (360,000 litre) 'reef tank', the world's largest, in which a coral reef and all its attendant marine life has been created. The park also offers a nature trail, turtle pools, shops, restaurant and souvenir shops, and the world's only 'underwater' mailbox, post from which gets a special postmark. Latest additions include two Sea World Explorers which give the views and sensations of submarine travel without having to dive beneath the surface. There are also tropical bird shows and aviaries. The park is open daily 9am to 6pm.

**Coki Beach** is a popular beach, especially when the cruise ships are in and passengers take an opportunity for a dip before or after visiting Coral World. There are usually lifeguards on duty, food is available and there is good snorkelling and diving in the bay.

You can then either return south on the twisting route 38 back to Charlotte Amalie, which will take about 30 minutes at a gentle pace. This road takes you through the mountains, and you stick to route 38 all the way through **Estate Tutu**

*Above and below: Discover the secrets of Coral World*

with its restaurant, Jim Tillet's Gardens and crafts workshops. The estate used to be a Danish cattle farm and is now noted for its silk screening studio and galleries featuring local artists and craftsmen. Jim Tillet is now semi-retired and in his 80s, but he still paints and creates new designs. You can also watch brilliant woodcarver Afreekan Southwell working. His preferred woods are lignum vitae and mahogany, and he is also an accomplished painter, poet and sculptor. During school holidays there are usually several children around the studio being encouraged and trained by him. The gardens are used for art and music festivals throughout the year.

Continue past the Four Winds Shopping Center and then along the Weymouth Rhymer Highway past the St. Thomas hospital, back into the capital.

To continue to explore the northern coast a little further west, head south a short way on route 38 before turning right on route 42 to continue along the northern coast past Tutu Bay and Mandal Bay on Mahogany Run Road. The road takes you past Winterberg Peak 977ft (298m), inland to your left.

The **Mahogany Run Golf Course** has to be one of the most scenic in the world, and if you have the chance to play, you can cool off afterwards in **Mandal Bay**, which is much quieter than the next few beaches further west.

Continue west to **Magens Bay**, a deep bay sheltered by a long thin promontory jutting out north-westwards into the sea protecting the bay's northern flank. Further north out to sea are the islands of Hans Lollik and just beyond, Little Hans Lollik. There is a road which takes you to the end of the promontory.

Magens Bay beach is hugely popular with visitors and islanders alike, and it is a great place to be at weekends and on public holidays when entire families turn out to picnic and swim. There are picnic benches and barbecue grills provided and the beach can get very crowded. The waters are usually very calm as the bay is protected on both sides by peninsulas which reach out into the sea. There are restaurants and snack bars and most watersport equipment is available for rent.

Inland, the arboretum is being restored by the local Rotary Club. There are signs identifying the different species. Also nearby are the remains of old Danish sugar mills. There is also the Magens Bay Educational Trail, which starts by the yellow office building at the entrance of the park. The trail winds through several habitats and passes a number of archaeological excavations and the arboretum. Signs also point out things of interest along the way.

From Magens Bay you return south on Magens Road to pick up route 35 for the drive back to Charlotte Amalie. On the way take the windy road up to visit **Drake's Seat** where, it is claimed, Sir Francis Drake posted look-outs to watch over his ships in the harbor, and to alert him of Spanish galleons out at sea. You can appreciate the vantage point the look-outs had, and if you visit Drake's Seat late in the afternoon as the sun starts to sink, the coast and sea is bathed in vivid purple, blue and pink colours.

Also on the drive back take in the **Skyline Drive**, which is appropriately named as it follows a mountain ridge and offers fantastic views over Charlotte Amalie, the harbor and surrounding countryside. It is also another great place to watch the spectacular sunsets as the great red ball of the sun dips into the sea. You can either drive the length of the Skyline Drive and return to Charlotte Amalie on route 38, or drive part of the route, and then return to route 35 for the drive back to Charlotte Amalie on the Mafolie Road, which brings you back into the city past Government Hill.

## EATING OUT ON THE EAST OF THE ISLAND

| Inexpensive | $ |
| Moderate | $$ |
| Expensive | $$$ |

**Agave Terrace** $$-$$$ Smith Bay, Award-winning restaurant with great seafood and continental specialities ☎ 775-4142

**Baron** $$ Watergate Villas, West Indian ☎ 775-9291.

**Birds of Paradise** $$ Saga Haven Marina, West Indian and Seafood ☎ 775-4747

**Brass Parrot Bar and Grill** $$ Magens Point Resort, Tex-Mex ☎ 775-5500

**Cafe Vecchio** $$ Grand Palazzo, Italian ☎ 775-3333.

**Caribbean Lobster House** $$ Limetree Beach, Seafood dinner ☎ 776-4770

**Daddy's** $$ Redhook, Seafood and Continental ☎ 775-6590

*Following pages: Cruz Bay*

**Eden Paradise Grill** $$ Secret Harbour, Seafood and Continental ☎ 775-6198. Good wine list. Reservations recommended.

**Eunice's Terrace** $-$$ Smith Bay, Great seafood and Creole ☎ 775-3975

**For The Birds** $$ Scotts Beach, Tex-Mex and barbecue ☎ 775-6431

**Iggie's** $$ Limetree Beach, ribs to pasta ☎ 776-4770

**Lord Rumbottom's** $$ Bolongo Beach, Steak and salad ☎ 775-1800.

**Mim's Seaside Bistro** $-$$ Watergate Villas, Seafood ☎ 775-2081

**Morgan's Mango** $$ Tillet Gardens, Caribbean with South American touches ☎ 775-4550

**Piccola Marina Cafe** $-$$ Redhook, Open air seafood restaurant by the ferry ☎ 775-6350

**Tickles Dockside Pub** $-$$ Redhook, American ☎ 775-9425

**Viola's Calypso Kitchen** $$ Bolongo Bay, West Indian ☎ 775-1800

**Wyndham Sugar Bay Resort** — *Mangrove's Cafe* $-$$ American, *Turtle Rock Bar* $-$$ American, *The Manor House* $$-$$$ Seafood and Continental ☎ 777-7100

# ST. JOHN

St. John is a delightful island whose peace and tranquillity today belies its bloody history. Peaceful Arawak Indians lived on the island as early as 700BC but were wiped out by the fearsome Caribs in the century before Columbus arrived. In the early eighteenth century, the island had scores of huge and wealthy estates, but almost all of the settlers and their families were murdered during the slave uprising in November, 1733. At the height of its prosperity, the island boasted 109 plantations.

Today, most of the island is a wonderful National Park, thanks to the donation of land by Laurance Rockefeller. The trees and vegetation have been allowed to reclaim the land. Many of the old plantation houses now lie in ruins, almost hidden by vegetation and flowering vines, but some survive and can still be visited, such as Annaberg and Caneel Bay. There are thirty-one fabulous beaches and bays offering white sandy beaches, safe swimming and excellent diving.

It is claimed that the island has such an equitable climate, that most people never catch a cold, and certainly the pace of life is very gentle. Most of the islanders are engaged in farming or fishing, and traditional crafts, such as weaving and charcoal burning. St. John Carnival takes place during the first week of July, and is the island's biggest event.

Traces of Carib settlements have been found and there are many rock paintings to be seen around the island. It is also not unusual to come across artifacts lying on the ground and long hidden by undergrowth. People have discovered old muskets, cannon balls and other items, and if you find something, report it to the rangers.

## CRUZ BAY

The island's port of entry is Cruz Bay, which is the main settlement on St. John with US Customs, post office, school, bank, shops and a US Ranger Station. It is where the ferries dock and the seaplanes land in the harbor, and where you pick up your hire car, jeep, taxi or tour bus. It is also the only place on the island where you can get fuel — there are now two filling stations on the outskirts. The settlement is so compact that some of the streets do not even have official names, but it does not matter as it is impossible to get lost.

When getting off the ferry, check the notice board at the end of the pier which has information about special events and other news for visitors, then turn left and follow the road round the bay to the ranger station and **National Park Visitor's Center**, which is on the north shore of the bay with its own dock, opposite the historic flag-flying Battery, which now houses the island's administrative offices. Park rangers organise a programme of talks, events and activities, and have a wealth of information on beaches, wildlife watching, hiking trails through the park and so on. It is also a good idea to take in the 18-minute orientation video. There are several trails which start from the visitor center. These include the 1½ mile (2km) trail from the visitor center to the site of the Lind Battery on Lind Point, built by the English, allegedly in just one night, during the Napoleonic Wars. The trail also

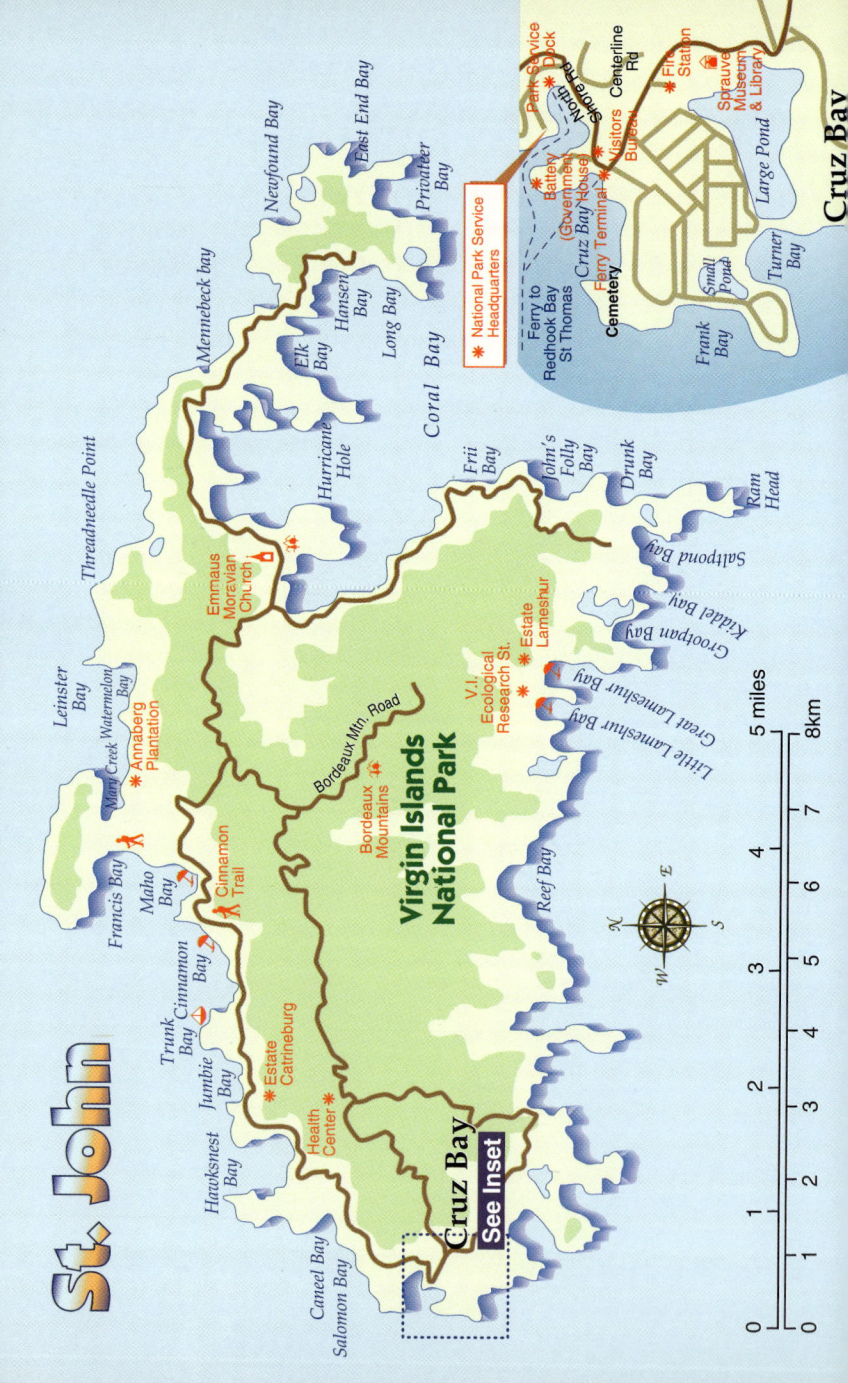

## GETTING THERE

By Sea: There is a daily ferry between Redhook on St. Thomas and Cruz Bay on St. John. The ferries run from early morning to late at night, and leave on the hour from both islands, and the crossing takes 20 minutes. During the St. John Carnival, the ferries are more frequent and often run until 2am. There is also a daily ferry service between Charlotte Amalie and Cruz Bay. There are six sailings a day between 9am and 7pm, and ferries leave Charlotte Amalie every 2 hours for the 30 minute crossing. Most of the ferries from St. John leave at 15 minutes past the hour.

By Air: There is a seaplane service between St. Thomas and St. John. The seaplanes operate from Cruz Bay on St. John.

## GETTING AROUND

Taxis are plentiful and not expensive if you share the ride. Many fares are fixed, but check first. Typial fares for two from Cruz Bay are Annaberg Plantation $12.50, Maho Bay $12.50, Trunk Bay $7.50, Salt Pond $20 and Caneel Bay $5. Taxis can also be hired for tours of the island and should charge about $30-35 for a couple of hours. Hire cars are also available, and jeeps are preferable as the main roads are not that good and the side roads worse. Drivers need to take great care because of the road conditions and other vehicles, especially water tankers and safari buses which serve as public transport.

There is a ferry between the National Park Service Dock and Caneel Bay which allows you to take a taxi to the park for a day's walking and then catch the ferry back. This ferry can be very busy so reserve a seat. There are also many safari bus and jeep tours of the park, and tour prices are fixed.

connects with the Caneel Trail which leads to one of the island's most beautiful beaches. There is also the Caneel Hill Trail which follows the high ground over Caneel Hill, Tamarind Tree and Margaret Hill to Caneel Bay. After a swim, you can then return along the coastal path. The center is open daily from 8am to 4.30pm. Armed with information, walk back into town past the US Customs offices and visit the **Battery**, built in 1735 during a period of great unrest on the island. It was constructed to provide a shelter for the townspeople in the event of further slave uprisings, and now has a small museum open Monday to Friday between 10am and 2pm. Admission is free. Most of the places to visit in Cruz Bay are contained within two blocks of the ferry dock, including shops, restaurants, banks, post office and police station. Close to the pier is the Nazareth Lutheran Church and across from the harbour is Gallows Point, scene of many public executions over the years.

Centerline Road runs virtually from the ferry dock across the island and through the mountains as route 10, to Coral Bay and then on to the eastern tip of the island.

On the outskirts of Cruz Bay the road forks with Southside Road (route 104) running off to the right by one of the island's only two filling stations, the other is about a ¼ mile (1km) further up the road. This road leads to the beaches on the south-west corner of the island and then swings inland to join the Centerline Road. A couple of hundred yards up South Shore Road from the junction on the left are the **Elaine Sprauve Library and St. John Museum**, both in a former mansion, built in 1735 but mostly rebuilt because of damage by fire and hurricane, and restored in 1982. The museum is open Monday to Friday from 9am to 5pm.

Just north of Cruz Bay is the **Moravian Bethany Mission** founded in 1754, and its eighteenth-century parish hall. In 1741, Jens Rasmus, a plantation overseer, invited the Moravians to come to the island to preach to the slaves on the estate where he worked. The church has been rebuilt three times after storm damage.

The St. John Community Health Center is further along Centerline Road. From Centerline Road there is a trail to **Estate Catrineberg**, one of the first plantations on the island and now completely overgrown although some buildings including the windmill and horsemill can be made out.

North Shore Road (route 20) runs west out of town past the Post

Office and the Mongoose Junction Shopping Center and leads to most of the beaches on the northern coastline, all within the National Park boundary, before connecting with Centerline Road near the Annaberg Plantation inland from Leinster Bay.

## AN ISLAND TOUR

This trip requires a four wheel drive vehicle for some of the roads, especially in the east of the island around the Bordeaux Mountain. Drive safely and on the left, and if you want to take photographs use one of the many pull-offs, specially built for this. The planners had a good eye for a picture, because all the pull-offs offer stunning views. Talking about photographs, there are a number of wild donkeys on the island which look photogenic — but they sometimes bite!

Take North Shore Road out of town which becomes route 20, and you immediately drive into one of the most spectacular stretches of coastline in the Caribbean, with magnificent beach after magnificent beach. There is **Salomon Bay** and **Caneel Bay** with its luxury resort which takes in part of the beach, although non guests are usually welcome to use it and the restaurants. Caneel Bay is really a series of seven white sand beaches, of which only one is public. The others do provide more facilities, such as restaurants and shops. There is also great diving off Caneel Bay, one of the prettiest on the island with its white, soft sand and coconut palm-fringed beaches. During the week there are boat trips from the bay to Virgin Gorda — they leave in the morning, include lunch on the island, and return late in the afternoon.

The magnificent **Caneel Bay Plantation Resort** was built by Laurance Rockefeller, around the former sugar cane estate and incorporating many of its old buildings. There are no televsions or telephones in the rooms scattered around the 170-acre (68 hectare) estate, and the aim is for guests to enjoy the sheer beauty of the land, that persuaded Rockefeller to make his home there. The gardens are very well tended and many of the plants and trees have identity tags. Offshore are Rata, Henley and Ramgoat Cays.

Next is the beautiful **Hawksnest Beach**, watched over by the huge concrete short-armed statue of Christ of the Caribbean on the cliffs, and popular with locals and many St. Thomians who like to holiday here. The armless statue was erected by Colonel Julius Wadsworth in 1953 and was donated to the island, together with

# CARIBBEAN SUNSEEKERS: US VIRGIN ISLANDS

the 9 acre (4 hectare) site on which it stands, in 1975. The area used to be part of the Denis Bay Plantation and the ruins of many of the old buildings can still be seen.

Then you pass the much smaller but equally lovely **Jumbie Bay**, which is reached down a very steep slope. **Trunk Beach** is next which offers excellent bathing and diving. It gets its name from the Trunkback, or leatherback turtles, which used to come ashore to lay their eggs in the sand. Offshore is **Trunk Bay** and in the waters between, is a marked underwater trail for snorkellers. Lifeguards are normally on duty and the long stretch of white sand is backed by shade providing palm trees. There is also a beach café.

Continue to the sweeping **Cinnamon Bay** with its fine public beach, the longest on the island, and nearby campsite whose facilities you can use. There are tent cottages, conventional tents and bare-sites. Inland here is the 1 mile (2km) **Cinnamon Trail** which leads through lush tropical vegetation, and passes the ruins of an old sugar mill. The Great House was destroyed by a hurricane in the early nineteenth century. Further along are several old charcoal points, used by English settlers who came from Tortola to fell the timber, and then the old Danish cemetery.

The three lovely beaches of **Maho Bay** are next, with its award-winning eco-campground. The campground is dedicated to preserving the environment, and has taken conservation and re-cycling to a fine art. Many of its innovations are world-beaters and have won international conservation awards. Boardwalks run everywhere so that people do not walk on the ground causing damage. Whenever possible, only re-cycled materials are used in construction. Harmony on the hill overlooking the bay has taken conservation camping even further, and with its sister camp Concordia on the south coast near Salt Pond, are the only ones in the world running only on solar and wind power.

Continue to **Francis Bay**, where there is a short trail through the scrub vegetation. There are many pelicans in this area, and both bays provide good snorkelling.

For four-wheel drive vehicles, the road continues along the coast past Mary Creek and Mary Point towards Leinster Bay, but our route cuts inland for the short drive to visit the **Annaberg Plantation** founded in

*Facing page, above: Caneel Bay*
*Facing page, below: Hawksnest Bay*

1780. This former huge 500 acre (200 hectares) Danish sugar estate with its mill has been partly restored by the Park Service. There is an excellent brochure to accompany the self-guiding trail on which you can learn all about the estate, how sugar was processed and what the various buildings were used for. The estate was bought by a cattle rancher at the beginning of the twentieth century but he built a wood house to live in, and used the old Danish buildings for his animals and stores. The estate is open daily during daylight hours and admission is free. Annaberg Plantation stands in Leinster Bay on the northern coast, and was the site of the last stand by the slaves after their 1733 uprising. A force of 400 French soldiers had chased the slaves northwards and encircled them at the Annaberg Plantation. The 300 slaves, rather than surrender, decided to commit mass suicide. Most of the men stabbed each other to death but a few men and most of the women and children, jumped over the cliffs on to the rocks below, and when the French did attack, they found no one alive. According to legend, some of the slaves plunged to their deaths off the Minna Neger Ghut cliff on Mary Point, which is the promontory to the north-west beyond Mary Creek. According to local legend, each year on the anniversary of the event, the waters below the cliffs turn red. There are some delightful short walks from Annaberg to Coral Bay. One follows the remains of the old Danish road.

Head back towards Maho Bay following the one-way system on route 20, and then join route 10 — Centerline Road — which runs between Cruz Bay and Coral Bay. Be alert for the small deer that frequent the woods in this area, and may stray on to the road. You can cut south and then west on this back to Cruz Bay, although our route continues eastwards.

Centerline Road runs parallel with the coast with Leinster Bay, Watermelon Cay, and Leinster and Threadneedle Points to your left on the eastern coast. There are several tracks down to the beaches along this stretch of coastline.

Inland to your right, the scenery is dominated by **Bordeaux Mountain** at 1,277ft (389m), and there are stunning views from the aptly named Picture Point eastwards over Coral Bay and across The Narrows to the British Virgin Islands. There are large stands of bay trees off the road. The aromatic leaves of the trees are crushed to extract the oil which is used to produce the famous St. John bay rum essences. **Estate Lameshur** can be reached by taking the rough Bordeaux Mountain Road (route 107), which runs south from Centerline Road down the western side of the mountains. The estate produces much of the island's oil, and some of the most well-known fragrances. You will appreciate why a four-wheel drive vehicle is needed to get to beautiful **Lameshur Bay** which has a great beach and clear waters for snorkelling. The unpaved road is very rough with large potholes, and your hire car company may specifically warn you against taking this route. If in doubt, you can park along the track and take the Bordeaux Mountain Trail which runs from the Bordeaux Mountain Road the 1.2 miles (2km) to the bay. There is 1,000ft (305m) of descent and the path is very exposed to the beating sun, so take care.

You can skirt south of the mountain on the unpaved roads using route 107 and then 108, which runs north-east to connect with the 107 again just south of Coral Bay.

Our route, however, continues on route 10 to **Coral Bay**, an enormous bay with many inlets and coves on the south-eastern edge of the island.

Coral Bay was the site of the earliest settlements on the island, including Estate Carolina, and there is evidence of Amerindian occupation dating back 2,000 years. The first Danish settlers in 1717 built Fort Frederik on the eastern shore of the bay, and it was seized by the slaves in 1733 and occupied by them for 6 months. At the foot of Fort Berg Hill, there is the site of an English Battery built during the Napoleonic Wars.

There is no reef in Coral Bay, which got its name from the Dutch word for 'corral', because the waters provided such a sheltered and safe anchorage. Admiral Horatio Nelson wrote that Coral Bay was the best anchorage in the Lesser Antilles, capable of accommodating up to 300 ships.

Despite the early settlements, Coral Bay was soon outshadowed by Cruz Bay, which developed because of its proximity to St. Thomas. Today Coral Bay is a small community with restaurants and bars, shops and private residences. The large, yellow Moravian church, built at the end of the eighteenth century, stands on the edge of the town, and the church is rumoured to be haunted by the spirits of a judge and his 12-year-old daughter murdered during the 1733 uprising.

*Following pages: Maho Beach*

The church and manse are on the National Register of Historic Places as one of the least altered Moravian complexes in the West Indies. The Mission House, although somewhat altered after storm damage and rebuilding, is largely the same building erected in the late eighteenth century. In 1993 it was fully restored and is now the home of the pastor and the parish meeting rooms.

Close by is the Moravian cemetery, and an old windmill.

A long narrow promontory runs along the northern edge of the bay, and this is worth exploring because of the many excellent beaches, and the rich bird life if you are interested in ornithology. As you drive east along the promontory, still on route 10 and clearly signposted, there is Coral Harbor on your right and then **Hurricane Hole**, named because it provides shelter for ships when there are storms at sea, with **Mennebeck Bay** shortly after on your left. Next on your right is **Round Bay** which includes **Elk Bay**, **Hansen Bay** and **Long Bay** where the road ends at East End. Just beyond Elk Bay the promontory narrows to just a few hundred feet in width, and this area is known as **Haulover**, presumably because it was the shortest distance to haul boats from the Atlantic Ocean to the south to the Caribbean on the north. Next on the northern coastline is **Newfound Bay** and on the easterly tip of the island, right at the end of the promontory and side by side, are **Privateer Bay** and **East End Bay**.

You have to return along the promontory, and then it is worth exploring the western side of the bay by driving south from Coral Bay on route 107 to **Ram Head**, the most southerly point on the island. Along this stretch of road you can visit **Johnson, Friis**, and **John's Foly Bays**, and **Drunk** (Creole for 'drowned') **Bay** which is just north of Ram Head. For part of the route, the road runs through **Estate Carolina**, once the Royal plantation of the King of Denmark. Just north of Ram Head, the road turns westwards and follows the southern shore of the island for a couple of miles before running out at Lameshur. This last section is only suitable for four-wheel drive vehicles. Along the way you pass the secluded **Saltpond Bay** and then **Kiddel, Grootpan** and **Great Lameshur Bays**. Just inland from Lameshur is the **Virgin Islands Ecological Research Station**. From Lameshur you can also walk north-west to visit Reef Bay Great house and the nearby petroglyphs, and then continue north to link up with Centerline Road, or you can take the trail south and walk to visit the ruins of the Reef Bay Sugar Factory near the bay.

If driving, you have to return almost back to Coral Bay to pick up Centerline Road. The journey west runs through the National Park which is a walker's and naturalist's paradise with scores of wild flowers and plants, many of them identified by signs, and a wealth of wildlife. There are many species of orchids, giant air plants, and exotic flowers, shrubs and trees, and more than a score of walking trails, all well maintained and posted. Many of the trails head off from Centerline Road, and while none of them are very long, some are quite strenuous because of the steepness of the terrain and the high temperatures. Sturdy footwear, hat and long trousers are recommended to avoid scratches and bites, and always carry a trail map which not only highlights all points of interest along the way, but also tells you what to be on guard against. Do not forget your swim gear and a towel, and as the water along the trails is not safe for drinking, always carry enough. A half gallon of water is recommended for each four hours walking in these temperatures and terrain. Always check in at one of the ranger stations before setting out, and check in on your return.

## PARK TRAILS
(courtesy of the Virgin Islands National Park)

Trail maps are available free from the National Park Visitor Center.

All trails are well waymarked, and laid out in such a way that you can combine several for longer hikes. * Trails marked with an asterisk lead to good snorkelling beaches.

### NORTH SHORE
**1.** Lind Point Trail 1.1 mile (1.7km) 1 hour *
Runs from the Visitor Center, Cruz Bay through cactus scrub and open dry forest to the secluded Honeymoon Beach at Caneel Bay, taking in the Lind Point Overlook at 160ft (49m). After three quarters of a mile (1.1km) there is a side trail to Salmomon Beach.

**2.** Caneel Hill Trail 2.4 miles (3.9km) 2 hours *
Starts in Cruz Bay and climbs for 0.8 mile (1.3km) out of the town to the top of Caneel Hill 719ft (219m), then to the summit of Margaret Hill 848ft (259m) before descending through forest to Northshore Road.

**3.** Caneel Hill Spur Trail 0.8 mile (1.3km) 40 minutes *
The trail starts from along the Lind Point Trail, crosses Northshore Road at the Cruz Bay/Caneel Bay

overlook and connects with the Caneel Hill Trail.

**4.** Water Catchment Trail 1 mile (1.6km) 30 minutes
The forest walk runs between Centerline and Northshore Roads, and follows the Caneel Hill trail for part of its route.

**5.** Turtle Point Trail 0.6 mile (1km) 30 minutes *
The trail starts at the north end of Caneel Bay Plantation and crosses private land by the tennis courts as it runs to the sea. Enter through the main gate and register at the front desk first.

**6.** Peace Hill 0.1 mile (0.16km) 10 minutes
The trail starts from the Northshore Road about 2.8 miles (4.5km) from Cruz Bay and leads to a viewpoint overlooking old sugar mills ruins and Hawksnest Beach with its statue of Christ of the Caribbean.

**7.** Cinnamon Bay Self Guiding Trail 0.5 miles (0.8km) 1 hour
A shady trail combining history and natural history, passing through the ruins of an old sugar factory and a stand of tropical trees. The trail starts just east of the entrance road to Cinnamon Bay campground.

**8.** Cinnamon Bay Trail 1.1 miles (1.8km) 1 hour
A forest trail which starts about 100 yards (90m) east of the entrance road to the campground. The trail follows an old Danish plantation road uphill to connect with Centerline Road, and from the road you can walk 0.9 miles (1.4km) east to connect with the Reef Bay Trail.

**9.** Francis Bay Trail 0.5 miles (0.8km) 30 minutes *
The trail starts at the west end of the Mary Creek paved road and passes through scrub forest and the historic Francis Bay Estate to the beach where you can explore a mangrove forest with its rich birdlife. There is a boardwalk to give better access to the pond and swamp areas. There are strong currents off shore, but inshore provides safe swimming and snorkelling.

**10.** Annaberg School Area 0.2 miles (0.3km) 15 minutes
The trail starts from the approach road to Maho Bay and leads to one of the island's oldest public school houses where there is a permanent historical exhibition. There are also fine views of Mary Point and Leinster Bay.

**11.** Annaberg Trail 0.2 miles (0.3km) 30 minutes

This trail explores the area by the Leinster Bay paved road where there are mangrove swamps and shallow reef flats rich in birdlife and land crabs. There is also a short self-guiding walk of the Annaberg Sugar Mill ruins just up from the picnic area. From the ruins there are fine views across to the British Virgin Islands.

**12.** Leinster Bay Trail 0.8 miles (1.3km) 30 minutes *
The trail follows the old Danish road east along the coast from the Annaberg picnic site to Watermelon Bay.

**13.** Johnny Horn Trail 1.8 miles (2.9km) 2 hours
This historic trail runs from Watermelon Bay across the hills to the paved road by the Moravian Church in Coral Bay. The trail is through scrub and is exposed to the sun.

**14.** Brown Bay Trail 1.6 miles (2.6km) 2 hours
One of the few unmaintained trails, and it starts about 0.7 miles (1.1km) along the Johnny Horn Trail from Watermelon Bay. It travels through scrub and a hot, exposed valley, bordering Brown Bay for a short distance and then climbing over the hill to overlook Hurricane Hole. It ends at the East End Road, 1.2 miles (1.9km) east of the Moravian Church at Coral Bay.

## SOUTH SHORE

**15.** Reef Bay Trail 2.2 miles (3.5km) 2 hours *
The trail begins just short of 5 miles (8km) from Cruz Bay on Centerline Road, and drops through both wet and dry forest, past the ruins of four sugar mills and other more recently abandoned farm buildings. There is a small picnic site and pit toilets near the Reef Bay sugar Mill close to the beach. Rangers also provide conducted hikes along this trail.

**16.** Petroglyph Trail 0.2 miles (0.3km) 15 minutes *
The trail runs from the Reef Bay Trail and offers the chance to see many Arawak rock carvings by the poolside.

**17.** Lameshur Bay Trail 1.5 miles (2.4km) 65 minutes
The trail runs between the Reef Bay Trail and Lameshur Bay. About 1.2 miles (1.9km) from the Reef Bay Trail junction, there is a small 0.3 mile (0.5km) detour to a salt pond and coral rubble beach at Europa Bay.

**18.** Yawzi Point Trail 0.3 miles (0.5km) 20 minutes
The trail starts close to the beach

from Little Lameshur Bay Road and runs through thorny scrub vegetation to the isolated cove by the point. People suffering from yaws, a highly contagious and disfiguring skin disease, were isolated here many years ago, thus its name.

**19.** Bordeaux Mountain Trail 1.2 miles (1.9km) 90 minutes
The exposed trail runs between Bordeaux Mountain Road and Lameshur Bay. It is 1,000ft (305m) down to the beach and the path can be very hot, especially on the return leg. From the Bordeaux Mountain Road end of the trail it is 1.7 miles (2.7km) north-west to Centerline Road.

**20.** Salt Pond Bay Trail 0.2 miles (0.3km) 15 minutes
The trail starts at the parking area 3.9 miles (6.3km) south of Coral Bay and runs down to the bay with its picnic area through arid cactus scrubland. This area is very hot and exposed, and hats and extra drinking water are recommended.

**21.** Drunk Bay Trail 0.3 miles (0.5km) 20 minutes
The trail starts at the south end of Salt Pond bay beach and follows the north side of the salt pond. During May and June accumulated salt on the edges of the pond is harvested by the islanders. The rocky Drunk Bay Beach is very exposed and windy which is why the vegetation is particularly stunted. Swimming is not advised here.

**22.** Ram Head Trail 1 mile (1.6km) 1 hour
The rocky, exposed trail starts at the south end of Salt Pond Bay beach and leads to a unique blue cobble beach before cutting up the 200ft (61m) hill which leads to a clifftop lookout. Care needs to be taken near the cliff edge.

The park covers almost 13,000 acres (5,200 hectares), although just over half of this includes the waters and reefs offshore. Rangers conduct several walks through the park and also lead snorkelling trips, and there is a programme of campfire activities, including slide shows, in the evenings. Binoculars are also a must and the new lightweight, miniature 8x20s or similar, are ideal. You can spot wading purple gallinules, hummingbirds and mangrove cuckoos, and around the coast watch diving pelicans and gliding frigate birds. Inland on the trails, be on the look out for mongoose, lizards and shy deer.

There are a number of rock carvings in the southern part of the park, and these can only be seen by hiking in along the Reef Bay Trail which is signposted off the Centerline Road, a mile or so west of Annaberg. The origin of some of the carvings is in doubt, with some attributed to the first African slaves, while others believe them to be of pre-Columbian origin and the work of Arawak or Carib Indians. The trail winds for 2½ miles (4km) down to the coast and takes you through the ruins of the Reef Bay Estate with its old sugar mills.

Head westwards about 1 mile (2km) past the Hammer Farm ruins until you reach the junction with the Southside Road and then turn left and follow it south to the coast. This road, also known as Gift Hill Road, is route 104, and runs around the south-west corner of the island back to Cruz Bay. There are several unpaved roads off the many bays and beaches in the area but exercise caution even in four wheel drive vehicles, as some of the slopes are very steep and there may not be room for turning at the bottom. Visit Rendezvous and Hart Bays and a number of even more secluded beaches to the east, such as Fish Bay and Genti Bay, but these are only accessible on foot along park trails. You can hike in to the ruins of the Reef Bay Estate and the petroglyphs from here as well.

The road then follows the coast westwards past Chocolate Hole, Great Cruz Bay with the luxury Virgin Grand Hotel, and Turner Bay, back into Cruz Bay. This south western corner of the island is outside the national park boundary, and there are many fine large homes on the headlands overlooking the water.

## EATING ON ST. JOHN

| Inexpensive | $ |
| Moderate | $$ |
| Expensive | $$$ |

**The Backyard** $ Cruz Bay, Fast food and bar snacks ☎ 776-8553

**Beni Iguana's Sushi Bar** $$-$$$ Cruz Bay, Japanese ☎ 779-4068

**Cafe Grand Restaurant** $$$ Hyatt Regency, fine dining ☎ 693-8000

**Cafe Roma** $-$$ Cruz Bay, Italian ☎ 776-6524

**Caneel Bay** $$-$$$ Choice of fine dining ☎ 776-6111

**Cap's** $ Famous Creole food stall near the dock. No telephone.

**Ciao Mein** $$-$$$ Hyatt Regency, Italian and Oriental ☎ 693-8000

**Coral View** $$$ near Coral Bay,

Seafood and snacks ☎ 776-6611

**Cruz Quarter** $$ Cruz Bay, Home cooking with hints of Tex-Mex ☎ 776-6908

**Don Carlos** $$ Coral Bay, Seafood and Mexican ☎ 776-6866

**Ellington's** $$-$$$ Gallows Point, light lunches and excellent West Indian-Polynesian dinners ☎ 776-7166

**Fishtrap** $$ Raintree Inn, Seafood ☎ 693-9994

**Fred's** $ Cruz Bay, Creole and seafood ☎ 776-6363

**Lime Inn** $$ Cruz Bay, Seafood specialities ☎ 776-6425

**Lucy's** $$ route 107, light lunches and tasty dinners, ☎ 776-6804

**Mongoose** $$ Mongoose Junction, American and Continental ☎ 776-7586

**Morgan's Mango** $$ Cruz Bay, Caribbean ☎ 693-8141

**Paradiso** $-$$ Mongoose Junction, Italian, ☎ 776-8806

**Pusser's Wharfside** $$ Wharfside Village, American ☎ 693-8489

**Old Gallery** $$-$$ Cruz Bay, Creole ☎ 776-7544

**Redbeard's** $ Centerline Road, Good fun and constantly changing menu ☎ 776-6665

**Saychelles** $$ Wharfside Village, West Indian and seafood ☎ 693-7030

**Seabreeze** $$ on route 107, Coral Bay, Seafood, open all day. No telephone

**Shipwreck Landing** $$ route 107, Coral Bay, Seafood and American fast food ☎ 776-8540

**Skinny Legs** $$ Cruz Bay, American grill ☎ 779-4982

**Sugar Mill** $$$ Caneel Bay, Seafood and Italian ☎ 776-6111

**Two Swans** $-$$ Cruz Bay, Snacks and light meals ☎ 776-7829

**Victor's New Hideout** $$ Cruz Bay, West Indian and Seafood ☎ 693-7225

*Facing page: Contessa's Castle*

**Vie's Snack Shack** $ East End, local specialities ☎ 776-8033

**Upper Deck** $$ off South Shore Road, Seafood and excellent meat, dinners only ☎ 776-6318.

**Woody's Seafood Saloon** $$ Cruz Bay, Seafood ☎ 779-4625

Lively bars include Beni Iguana and Wharfside Village, both in Cruz Bay.

# ST. CROIX

St. Croix (pronounced St. Croy), the 'Garden of the Antilles', is the largest of the US Virgin Islands and for centuries has been largely agricultural with almost all the available land under cultivation for sugar cane, and more recently for rearing cattle. The island boasts many fine old houses, and at the height of its prosperity, there were about 140 plantation houses, and more than 27,000 slaves. Old plantation houses and sugar mill ruins dot the island. The island is still sub-divided into the plots of land which represented each of the plantations, and these still carry their original names such as Little Princess, Bellevue, Wheel of Fortune, Jealousy, Solitude, Parasol and so on. When a plantation's name ends with the word 'Rest', it usually denotes that members of the family are buried on it in eternal rest.

Although it was the last island to become a Danish possession, it has retained more of its Danish heritage than either St. Thomas or St. John, and this is particularly evident in Christiansted, which was laid out in 1735, and although some of the city was ravaged by fire in 1866, many of the original buildings as well as the original layout survived.

The island was very badly hit by Hurricane Hugo in October 1989, and many of the islanders lost their homes during the onslaught of 240 mile (387km) an hour winds. Many of the historic buildings, however, escaped serious damage, and a major rebuilding programme over the past few years, has repaired much of the obvious damage caused by the storm.

The eastern end of the island is rocky and arid with mainly scrub and cacti vegetation, while the western end, which receives a much higher rainfall, is lush with forests. The area between is mostly rolling hills and open countryside. The north-eastern coast, in particular, is noted for its fine beaches, and the island boasts several international class golf courses. The A. Hamilton International Airport is on the south coast.

The island has changed hands many times over the centuries and six nations have ruled it at one time or another — Spain, Holland, France, England, Denmark and the United States — as well as the Knights of Malta, who established a community after buying the island from the French crown.

The Arawaks and then the Caribs were settlers on the island, and while little remains of the Carib culture, the remains of more than 120 Arawak settlements have been located during archaeological excavations, and their rock carvings have been found on stone slabs along the salt River, where Columbus is reputed to have sent ashore a landing party in 1493.

The Carib name for the island was Cibuquiera (Stony Land) but for a long time many people thought it was 'Ay Ay' because of a misunderstanding. When Columbus anchored in Salt River Bay, he pointed at the island and asked his Taino Indian guides where he was. They replied Ay Ay which was the Carib word for river, which is what they thought he was pointing at. Columbus re-named the island Santa Cruz and the French translated this to St. Croix.

## CHRISTIANSTED

**Note**: In both Christiansted and Frederiksted, street numbers are consecutive up one side and then back down the other, not odd and even as usually found elsewhere.

For many years Christiansted was the capital of the Danish Virgin Islands, and some areas have changed little since those days. The town was founded on the site of the older French settlement of Bassin. The small island capital has enormous charm with its historic port area, protected by offshore reefs, and many eighteenth-century buildings. Christiansted did not suffer as many fires as Frederiksted and towns on neighbouring islands because all building had to comply with rigorous fire-prevention rules introduced in 1747 which banned wooden roofs in favour of tiles and slates, and called for wide streets to prevent flames jumping.

The entire waterfront and town square is now a National Historic

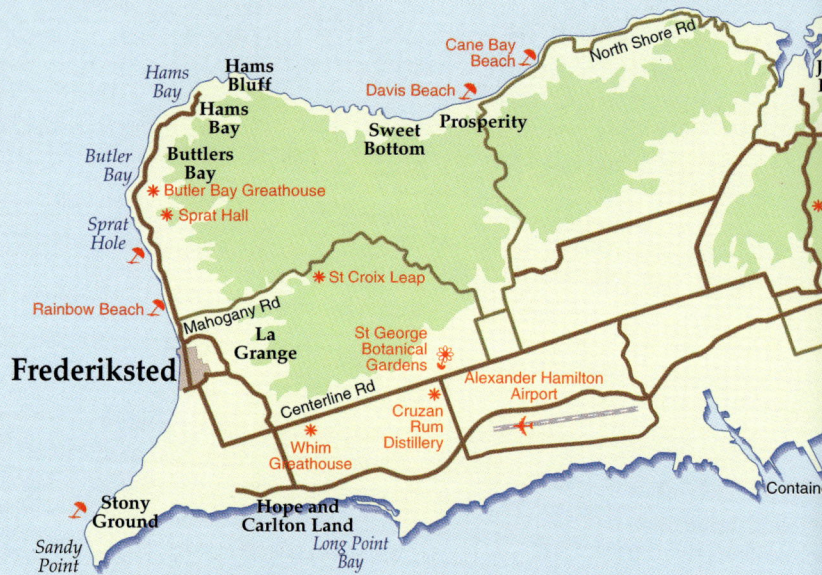

Site, maintained by the US National Park Service to reflect the building styles of the first half of the nineteenth century. There are four types of buildings in the town — public buildings, churches and Government offices, two and three storey brick built residences of wealthy merchants, two storey shopkeepers homes, who lived above the premises, and workers' homes, which tend to be one storey wooden shacks on the outskirts of town.

Running from the square there are streets and arcades with fascinating shops and eating places. There are also hotels and nightspots and the whole town is a blaze of colour, not just from the flowers that grow profusely everywhere, but the multi-coloured buildings as well.

The historic **Scale House** on the waterfront makes a good place to start your walking tour of the town, as it is also the Tourist Information Bureau and Post Office. Built in the mid-1850s, the Scale House was responsible for weighing all goods imported or exported from the port to ensure the correct custom duty was

paid. Across the parking lot are the former offices and warehouse of the Danish West Indian and Guinea Company, which now house a bank, shops and restaurant.

Across the road is the old Danish **Post Office** and **Customs House**, where the taxes were collected. The oldest part of the building dates from 1734 although several additions have been made. The first floor was enlarged in 1751 and most of the present extensions were added in the late 1820s. It was the town library from 1927,

and today houses offices, the National Park Service's Visitors' Center and an art gallery.

**Fort Christianvaern**, lies across Hamilton Jackson Park from the Scale House, and is the best preserved of the five forts built by the Danes on the islands. It is a remarkable structure with tiny, threatening dungeons, cannon and fortifications, and took 11 years to build, being completed in 1749, although its cannon were never fired in anger. It was built on the site of a French fort. Troops were stationed there until 1878. The yellow bricks used in the construction were shipped across the Atlantic as ballast in the trading ships which returned to Europe laden with sugar cane, cotton and rum. The fort still has an impressive arsenal of weapons. The 18-pounders date from 1692 and the six-pounders from 1834. The average 18 pounder barrel weighs 4,550 lbs (2048kg), and the six-pounder barrel 700lbs (315kg). The fort is now the headquarters for the US National Park Service in the Virgin Islands, and is open Monday to Friday 8am to 5pm and at weekends between 9am and 5pm. There is a leaflet for the self-guiding tour. The small admission charge also covers admission to the **Steeple Building**, which is just inland in Company Street, between Hospital and Church Streets. Originally the Church of our Lord of Sabaoth, it was the first Lutheran Church on the islands, and was finished in 1753 replacing a 1734 structure. The Georgian steeple was added at the end of the eighteenth century, and the building was acquired by the Government in 1831. It became known as the Steeple Building, and has been used as a school, hospital and military bakery. It was restored to its 1800 appearance in the 1960s. It is now a museum with Arawak and Carib artifacts, and displays about the island's sugar cane history. There is also a display which chronicles the black history of the Virgin Islands, and another that illustrates the many architectural styles to be seen. It is open weekdays 9am to 4pm and Saturday morning.

On the other side of the street are the former headquarters and stores of the Danish West India and Guinea Company, which are now used by the US Customs Service and Postal Service. The building dates from 1749 but was added to in the 1750s. Also in Company Street is **Apothecary Hall**, which was built in the eighteenth century as the city's pharmacy, and now contains offices, shops and eateries. **Markoe House**, 17 Church Street, is a good example of a large town house on three storeys with a seven bay façade, and **Mahogany Inn** at number 56, is a 'U'shaped brick building with inner courtyard, featuring an arched arcade façade.

Continue up Company Street one block to Queen Cross Street and the old **Market Place** on your left. It dates from the 1750's, and is still used to sell locally grown fruit and vegetables. The well was built in 1863.

Then retrace your route a short way and turn left into Queen Cross Street and walk to its junction with King Street (Kongens

Gade) and the **Lord God of Sabaoth Lutheran Church**, built originally in the 1740s as a Dutch Reform Church. The Lutherans took over the church when they decided to move from the Steeple Building in 1831. The neo-Classical tower was added in 1834.

Across from Queen Cross Street in King Street is **Government House** with its impressive yellow façade and arches. It is one of the finest Danish-style buildings on the islands. It was built in 1747 as a private dwelling, although there are more recent additions, and the present structure is really two buildings that were joined. The oldest parts are believed to date from 1747 and can be seen from King Street, and the building was converted for Government use in 1771. It is approached by an impressive flight of brick steps added in 1830. It has a magnificent ballroom, traditional kitchen, and fine collection of Danish furniture and furnishings, donated by the Danish Government in 1966. It is now used for administrative offices, but you can go in and walk up the sweeping staircase to the ballroom.

In King Street is the site of the Cruger **'Alexander Hamilton' House**, the hardware shop where, when aged 11, he worked as a clerk. The building dates from 1750 but was rebuilt after being destoyed by a fire in the 1960s. Hamilton was born on Nevis but soon moved with his mother to St. Croix. He went on to become one of the leaders in the American Revolution. He was also appointed by Washington the first US Secretary of Treasury, which is why his portrait now graces every $10 bill. Other good examples of traditional architecture can be seen at 67 East Street, a two-storey masonry and wood structure, Solhoj at 4-5 Hill Street, reached by a long flight of steps, and Bjerget, 56-58 Hill Street, one of the finest town houses on the island. In Queen Street (note: entrance is on Company Street) is the Holy Cross Catholic Church built originally in 1755 and replaced by the present structure in the 1850s. It is a mix of Gothic and neo-Classical with elaborate cornices and pinnacles.

The main shopping area is around King Street and there are many intriguing little alleys to explore off it. Also in King Street is the **Florence A. Williams Library**, which has a fine collection of books on St. Croix and the Caribbean. The Pentheny Hotel at 46 King Street, is built round an inner courtyard. Originally a private residence, it became a hotel and is now offices. The Gothic Revival **St. John's**

## GETTING AROUND

There are excellent walking trails, bicycles for hire, and there are also horses and donkeys for hire for those who want a more leisurely mode of transport. Road conditions vary enormously around the island, and if you plan to do a lot of driving and exploration, hire a four-wheel drive vehicle. The main roads, however, are very good and are much quieter than on St. Thomas.

Taxis are not metered but there are set fares for most routes, and drivers must carry a list of these. The fares are also available at the airport and hotels. It is always a good idea, however, to agree the fare before setting off. There are extra charges for luggage, late night travel and waiting. It is quite common for someone to wave down your cab and hop aboard, so do the same as it is a good way of cutting down the fare. If you do not want to hire a car, taxi drivers make excellent island guides and their vehicles can be hired by the hour or longer. Expect to pay around $20-25 an hour. There is a bus service between Christiansted and Frederiksted.

If you enjoy walking, the St. Croix Environmental Association (☎ 773-1989), based in Apothecary Courtyard, Company Street, Christiansted, organises an extensive programme of island nature hikes. Their information office and gift shop is open Monday to Friday.

For island hopping day trips by air, there is Bohlke International Airways ☎ 778-9177 which flies from St. Croix to St. Thomas, Virgin Gorda in the British Virgin Islands, French St. Barts and Barbados.

**Anglican Church**, built in 1849, is the third church on the site, and further along, the 1854 **Friedensthal Moravian Church**, both on the outskirts of town, on the continuation of the road as route 72, also called Midland Road. The Moravian Church was built in sections in Germany in the nineteenth century and shipped to St. Croix for assembly.

Inland is Grange Road which leads to the ruins of **Estate Grange** to the east of Frederiksted, where there is a monument to Rachel Levine, mother of Alexander Hamilton. She is buried in an unmarked grave somewhere on the estate. There is also a monument to Danish soldiers who died there in 1866 when the estate was used as an isolation hospital during an outbreak of yellow fever in the nearby town. Today the great house is a private residence. Also close by are the ruins of Estate Anna's Hope.

**Protestant Cay** stands in the harbour, and has a hotel and fine beach and is a good place to rent sail boats. The island gets its name from the time when the French were in control of St. Croix, Catholicism was the only religion allowed and Protestants were refused church burial, so their dead were taken to this small island were funeral services were held.

The island makes a great day out and is only a couple of minutes from Christiansted. You can take a picnic or eat on the island, and can rent loungers or watersport equipment.

## EATING OUT IN AND AROUND CHRISTIANSTED

| Inexpensive | $ |
| Moderate | $$ |
| Expensive | $$$ |

**Anabelle's Tea Room** $-$$ Cuban, Hispanic, Spanish and local. A delightful courtyard setting. Try the Conch Bell, the only conch 'sandwich' on the island.
☎ 773-3990

**Antoine's** $$ Anchor Inn, Seafood and Swiss ☎ 773-0263

**Banana Bay Club** $-$$ Caravelle Hotel, hot sandwiches, burgers and daily specials, open all day
☎ 778-9110

**Bombay Club** $$ King Street, Creole, American and Indian
☎ 733-1838

**Brady's** $$ Hill Street, West Indian ☎ 773-2505

**Buccaneer: Little Mermaid Restaurant** $-$$ Continental and light lunches, Grotto $ sandwiches and snacks, Brass Parrot $$-$$$ International, The Terrace $-$$$ breakfast and dinner ☎ 773-2100

**Cafe Christine** $$ Company Street, French cuisine and pasta
☎ 773-9649

**Camille's** $$ Company Street, hot and cold sandwiches, salads
☎ 773-2985

**Captain's Table** $$$ Company Street, Seafood specialities
☎ 773-4532

**Chart House** $$ King's Wharf, Seafood and international
☎ 773-7718

**Chenay Bay Beach Club** $$ relaxed American, Creole and Crucian, entertainment several nights. ☎ 773-2918. Enjoy the West Indian pig roast on Tuesday, but reserve your seat.

**Club Comanche** $$ Strand Street, Creole and American and fabulous curries ☎ 73-2665

**China Jade** $-$$ Sion Farm Shopping Centre, Chinese
☎ 778-1996

**Cormorant Beach Club** $$$ Pelican Cove, excellent Island specialities and continental
☎ 778-8920. Try the lobster.

**Dimitri Ristorante** $$ Princess Plaza, Italian and pizza
☎ 773-1100

**Dino's** $-$$ Hospital Street, Italian
☎ 778-8005

**Galleon** $$ Green Cay Marina, very good French and Continental
☎ 773-9949

**Hamilton Mews** $-$$ King's Alley, Snacks and light meals
☎ 773-6450

**Harvey's** $$ Company Street, Great Creole ☎ 773-3433

**Jackie's East** $ 4 King Street, Fast food Cruzen-style ☎ 778-8160

**Indies** $$-$$$ Company Street, Excellent island cuisine, reservations recommended
☎ 692-9440

**Kendricks** $$-$$$ King Street, Elegant American-European
☎ 773-9199. Great lobster with pepper puree and rosemary pesto sauce, or try the roasted pecan crusted pork loin à la O'Brien, or the grilled fresh breast of duck with molasses.

**King's Alley Cafe** $$ King's Alley, American ☎ 773-0468

**Oskar's** $$ La Grande Princess, American-Eastern European ☎ 773-4060

**Lizards** $-$$ Strand Street, Fun Island fare ☎ 773-4485. Try the iguano ribs or gecko ribs!

**Luncheria Mexican** $$ Company Street, Mexican food and drink ☎ 773-4247

**Midland** $ King Hill, Cruzan cooking ☎ 778-0979

**Stixx on the Waterfront** $$ Pan Am Pavilion, International ☎ 773-5157

**Tivoli Gardens** $$ Pan Am Pavilion, International ☎ 773-2346

**Tommy and Susan's Taverna** $-$$ lively Greek ☎ 773-8666

**Top Hat** $$-$$$ Company Street, Excellent International and Danish specialities ☎ 773-2346

**Tutto Bene** $$-$$$ Company Street, Italian ☎ 773-5229

**Under the Tamarind** $-$$ Market Square, Vegetarian ☎ 773-0587

## THE WESTERN TOUR

Take route 75, the west coastal road out of Christiansted to pretty **St. Croix-by-the-Sea**, one of the many beach resorts along this beautiful stretch of coastline. There are a number of old estates along this stretch of road with wonderful names such as Little Princess and Golden Rock, and some fine beaches, including the long stretch of tree-lined **Pelican Cove** with its fine beach and Cormorant Beach Club. The reef offshore is popular with snorkellers.

Continue west along the coast then right on routes 751 or 79 to visit **Judith Fancy**, which it is claimed was modelled on a French château, and was the largest plantation on the island. It was built around 1660 by Governor du Bois, and was later the headquarters and the home of the Governor of the Knights of Malta, after they bought the island from the King of France. Although now largely in ruins, one mid-eighteenth century tower still remains intact and you can still see how impressive the house and out buildings must have been. The 'Judith' who has her name to the property was Judith Heyliger, born in 1672, who is buried on the estate close to the great house where her tombstone can be seen. The plantation which

## SALT RIVER NATIONAL PARK

According to William F. Cissel of the National Park Service in St. Croix, the Sat River National Park is important because it contains evidence of almost continuous occupation dating from AD300. The confrontation on 14 November, 1493 was also the first documented Native American resistance to European encroachment. The first settlers were the Igneri (Pre-Taino) and then the Taino Indians from Puerto Rico, and Salt River became an important settlement and religious and cultural centre. The only Tainan ceremonial ball court in the Lesser Antilles was unearthed here in 1923. Artifacts including human sacrificial burials, are on display in the National Museum in Copenhagen but may one day, be returned to St. Croix.

The Arawaks from South America then settled in the bay but were ousted by the Caribs around 1425. In 1509 Juan Ponce de Leon, the first Governor of Puerto Rico, made a deal with the St. Croix Caribs at Salt River. They pledged to stop attacking Puerto Rico and agreed to embrace Christianity and supply Puerto Rico with produce. Although de Leon had many slaves, he preferred them to work in the gold and silver mines rather than on the land. The Spanish broke their promise to leave the Caribs alone, raided the island and took away 140 Caribs as slaves. The caribs attacked Puerto Rico and in 1511 the Sanish King ordered that all Caribs everywhere be hunted down and killed. By 1590 all the Caribs had fled or slain. From around 1640 there were many attempts to settle around Salt Bay by the English, Dutch, French and Knights of Malta. In 1641 the English started work on an earthwork fortification which can still be seen on the west bank of the river. In the 18th and 19th centuries, Salt River Bay was used as an anchorage for ships loading sugar, rum and molasses from the many plantations inland, and a small cannon battery and Customs House was built by the Danes to protect this trade. Today the area is protected and considered so important, it may be declared a World Heritage Site.

was producing sugar cane more than 300 years ago, overlooks the broad mouth of the Salt River and Sugar Bay where ships used to anchor to take on board the plantation's crops. You reach it by returning to route 75 then turning right on route 80 and driving about one mile (1.6km) past the Salt River Marina.

Columbus anchored at the mouth of the river on 14 November, 1493 and sent ashore a party to collect freshwater. Although his men attacked but were repelled by the Caribs who lived along the river, Columbus claimed the island for Spain and called it Santa Cruz. In 1993, on the 500th anniversary of Columbus' arrival at Salt River, the landing site and surrounding 912-acre (365 hectare) area were declared a National Park. There is a marker on the left near the beach commemorating the historic landing. **Salt River Bay** offers some of the best reef diving on the island. It is noted for its plate coral covered precipices, huge sponges and large shoals of fish. In Salt Bay there is the wreck of the freighter *Cumulus*, which foundered on the reefs in October 1977, carrying a cargo of stolen cars.

Take the North Shore Road (route 80) along the north coast, and this route continues as the Scenic Road (route 78). A four wheel drive vehicle is really needed for this route. To the south is Betsy's Jewel and Eagle Mountain with Blue Mountain 1,096ft (334m). lurking behind it. Eagle Mountain 1,165ft (355m) is the island's highest peak, and the scenic road passes close by the summit.

The road passes the ruins of Estate Rust-Op-Twist (Rest After Work), which was later the site of an experimental shrimp farm, and at the village of La Vallee, you turn right for **Cane Bay** which offers wonderful views both above and below the water. The palm-fringed bay is protected by a reef and coral garden and teems with marine life, although the waves are often big enough for surfing. There is a sea wall which plunges 2,000 feet (610m) below the surface.

A little further west the road forks and there are a number of options. The road inland (route 69) leads to the Fountain Valley and the Carambala Golf Course, and there are a number of feeder roads off this leading to old plantation sites, such as Sweet Bottom, Prosperity, and Bonne Esperance which nestle in the hills. The roads, however, are not good and are best negotiated in a four-wheel drive vehicle. The area is worth exploring, however, because of the views and the lush tropical vegetation, and as the hills rise to more than 1,000ft (305m) above sea level, it is usually a few degrees cooler than at the coast.

Our route, however, continues along the scenic route which follows the north-west coastline to **Davis Bay**, which is part of the **Carambola Resort** with its championship golf course mentioned above but some way inland. There is limited access to the resort. The white sandy beach is fringed with palms, and the sea is popular with body surfers.

Round Hams Bluff, route 63 travels down the western side of the island to Butler Bay and **Sprat Hall**. The area around **Butler's Bay Greathouse** is known for its massive Baobab trees, which originally came from Madagascar. Legend has it that its strange shape is because a demon pulled up a baobab and stuck it back in the ground upside down with its roots in the air. The waters off Butler Bay are popular with divers because there are many wrecks. Three wrecks including the 177ft (54m) *Rosamaria* make up an artificial reef in the bay.

**Sprat Hall Beach** is almost 1 mile (2km) long and is accessible for a nominal charge. It is a great place for spotting the many differerent types of sea shells in the sand. There are Horse Stables at nearby **Sprat Hall Plantation** and you can ride on the beach or go on an escorted trail ride.

The road to Frederiksted runs through a small area of rain forest, about 15 acres (6 hectares), which extends north and east of the town, and while these areas are privately owned and not generally open to the public, the roads that run through them can be used to explore this region. Mahogany Road, or route 76, is one such route, and gets its name because of the mahogany trees that were planted on either side of the highway. You will also see yellow cedar, red-barked turpentine and Thibet trees planted between the mahogany. The Thibet tree is also known as 'mother's tongue' because the long pods rattle in the wind making a non-stop clatter! The road passes the Stone Quarry and and then a little way further up the road on the left is the entrance to the **St. Croix Leap**, which gets its name from the Life and Environmental Arts Project. Here you can watch many very talented woodcarvers at work using the local mahogany wood, and you can buy sculptured gifts and furniture which can be shipped home for you.

You can also take Creque (pronounced 'creaky') Dam Road — route 58 — which leads from Sprat Hall to the 150ft (46m) high dam, on the edge of the forest. There are also a number of trails

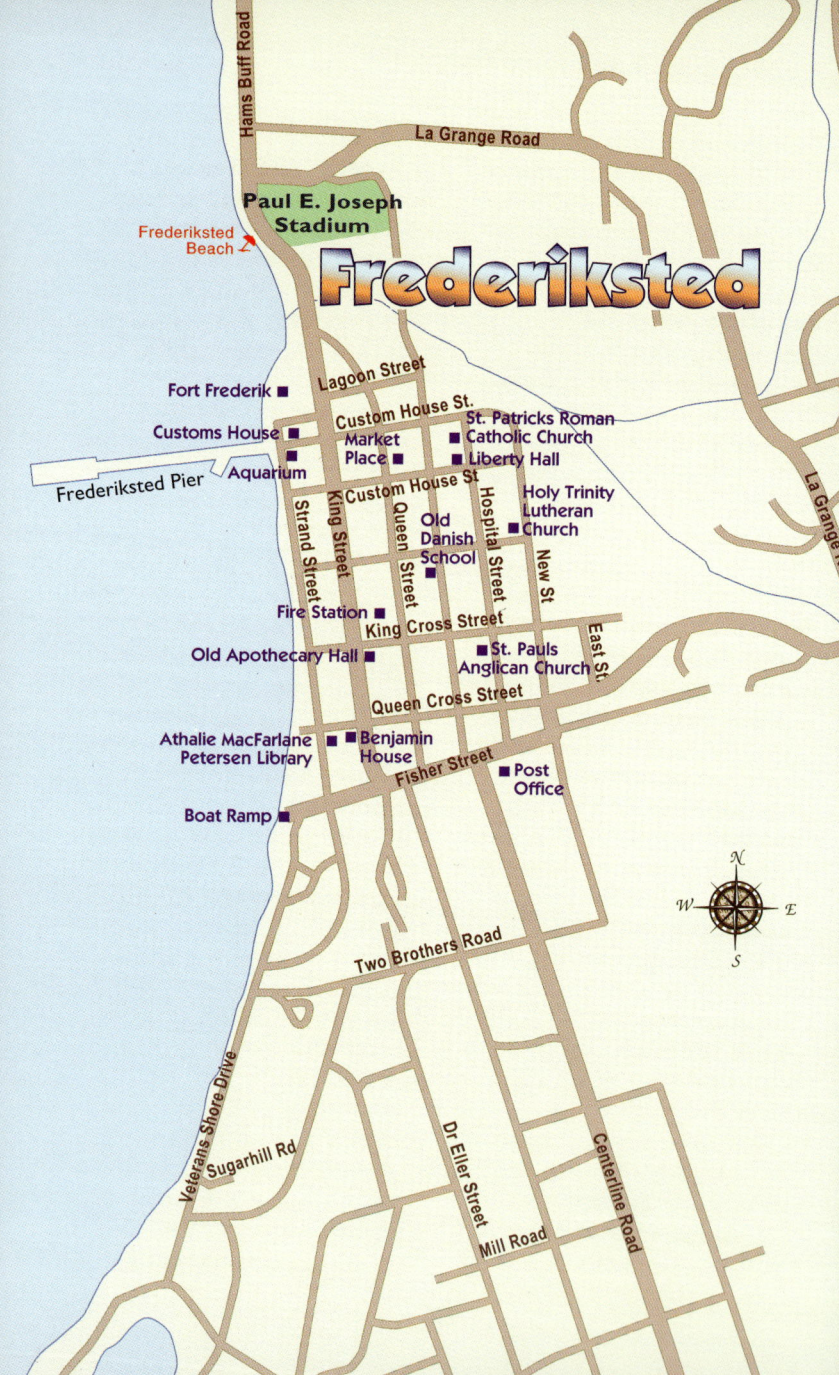

through the forests that can be walked which offer the chance of seeing the vegetation and widlife close to. Route 58 then connects with the Scenic Road.

North of Frederiksted is the brilliant white sand **Rainbow Beach**, which attracts snorkellers and seashell collectors, and at La Grange there is a small bar and you can relax on rented loungers.

## FREDERIKSTED

Frederiksted was established in 1751, and is the second town of the island on the western coast. Its growth was slow and in 1760 there was only a fort and two houses. By 1780 King and Queen Streets had been developed, and the Strand followed. In 1867 the town was almost wiped out by a massive tidal wave, and it was largely rebuilt after a massive fire in 1878. The fire was started deliberately and followed rioting by the families of the former slaves, provoked by their poor living conditions and wages. Most workers received only a few cents for a day's work. October 1 is still celebrated as Fireburn Day, in memory of Queen Mary, the labourer who led the fiery revolt.

The town that emerged is very Victorian in layout but with a variety of architectural styles as builders tried to recapture the character of the original. There are Colonial and Danish-style buildings with lots of Baroque and Gothic embellishments, although many of the buildings also incorporate traditional West Indian gingerbread features and wrought iron balconies. The town was badly hit by Hurricane Hugo, but most of the damage has been repaired. The cruise ship pier was destroyed, and has now been replaced with a new facility. Frederiksted really developed because of its fine harbor, and for centuries has played host to large vessels from around the world. The town is easy to explore on foot as most of the points of interest and shops are contained in a few blocks on the waterfront.

Start at the **tourist information center**, housed in the former **Customs House** by the pier at the end of Custom Street. The building dates from the late eighteenth century, although the gallery was added in the nineteenth century.

A short distance away is **Fort Frederik**, named after Danish King Frederik V, which was started in the early 1750s but not completed until 1760. In 1776 Denmark became the first foreign country to salute the flag of the newly created United States, when a US merchant vessel entered Frederiksted harbour and a salute was fired from Fort Frederik as the US flag was raised aboard. On 3 July 1848, it was where the proclamation abolishing slavery in the Danish West Indies was read by Governor General Peter Von Scholten. The fort was built to protect the large natural and sheltered harbour, and it is still used as an anchorage by most of the cruise ships visiting the island. The fort underwent many changes, and has recently been rebuilt with red and white brick to look as it did in the early nineteenth century, with barracks, stables, canteen and courtyard. It is now a museum, and art exhibitions are staged in the old garrison building. It is open weekdays.

South along the waterfront is Strand Street and on the corner with Market Street is **Victoria House**, which has long been a landmark. The original structure was built in 1803 but destroyed in the 1878 fire, and the Victorian structure erected on the site is a classic gingerbread design with its elaborate fretwork and scrolls. It is still a private home, and has been restored following damage by Hurricane Hugo. On the corner of Custom House Street and King Street is the **Fleming Building**, typical of the large commercial structures erected after the 1878 fire. The gable has an interesting sawn bargeboard. Also visit the **St. Croix Aquarium** on Strand Street and facing the pier, where you can learn about the island's marine life. The aquarium has a policy of constantly changing its displays so that all marine life exhibits do not spend too long in captivity.

Also in Strand Street on the corner of Queen Cross Street is the **Old Library**, the earliest parts of which date from 1803. It is now the arts and crafts center and houses the Dorsch Cultural Center for the Performing Arts. It is often referred to by islanders as the Bell House, because of a nineteenth-century owner named G.A. Bell who fitted bells over the central staircase. This charming waterfront area has many shops and cafés which offer excellent vantage points for spectacular sunsets.

Walk down Queen Cross Street to visit **Benjamin House** (number 48), a fine example of early nineteenth-century Danish residential design, and then left into King Street to visit the **Old Apothecary Hall**, on the corner with King Cross Street. It was built in the mid-nineteenth century and was one of the few buildings to survive the fire. It is a fine example of what the other buildings must have looked like before the fire.

Continue down King Cross Street to Prince Street and the Gothic **St. Paul's Episcopal Church**, built in 1812. The church Congregation dates back to the eighteenth century, and was orginally founded as Anglican and part of the Church of England, but 'converted' to become part of the Episcopal Church when the United States bought the Virgin Islands in 1917. The English Gothic tower was added in 1848. The **Holy Trinity Lutheran Church** dates from the late eighteenth century.

Head up Prince Street for the **Old Danish School**, which dates from the early 1830s, and was designed by the noted Danish architect Hingleberg. It is now part of the Ingeborg Nesbitt Clinic, and then continue past the junction with Market Street, to visit the coral-stone built **St. Patrick's Roman Catholic Cathedral Church**, completed in 1843 and dedicated on 23 June 1844. The limestone building with brick linings has undergone many changes, but its original cruciform design remains. The three-storey brick bell tower is a later addition, and the whole structure has a Spanish mission look. Cross over the road and into Market Street for the **Old Market**, which has been on the same site since the late 1700s. Turn left into Queen Street down to Hill Street and then left again for two blocks to visit the **Friedensborg Moravian Mission**, which was originally built in 1774. The present manse dates from 1852.

From Frederiksted continue south on route 70 and then turn right along the coast road which runs west past Westend Saltpond to the dunes at **Sandy Point**. There are many fine beaches to be explored along this coastline, which stretch the whole length of the western side of the island from Hams Bay to Sandy Point although many are only accessible on foot. Do not let the name **Stony Ground** put you off, because this is a fine beach, not far from town, with a sea water pool. This stretch of coastline is frequented by leatherneck turtles which haul themselves ashore between May and early July to lay their eggs in the sand.

Then take the Centerline Road, also known as the Queen Mary Highway (route 70), which runs east parallel with the south coast. Just south of the road is **Whim Greathouse**, built in 1794 and originally called John's Rest. It has been faithfully restored by the St. Croix Landmarks Society to depict

*Following pages: Old Sugar Mill, St Croix*

life on the island at the end of the nineteenth century. The house, surrounded by a moat, has period furnishings, silver and china and the walls, nearly 3ft (1m) thick, are made of stone and coral held together with a mortar made from molasses and lime. There is a reconstructed working windmill which was used to crush the sugar cane to extract the juices for distillation to rum, and there is a plantation museum, with equipment used in the cane crushing, juice boiling and rum distillation. Other exhibits include tools and household implements, military equipment, prints and carriages, and the tombstone of Anna Heegaard, daughter of a freed slave, and consort of Governor Von Scholten, who signed the decree freeing the slaves. The estate is also used as the venue for many cultural events including art shows and concerts. The museum is open Monday to Saturday between 10am and 5pm. There is a small admission charge. The Landmarks Society organises open house tours during the spring which allow visitors to see some of the great homes not normally open to the public. The estate has many old trees including tamarind trees at least 150 years old, mahogany and thibet.

To the south is **Long Point Bay** and **Betty's Hope**, which can be reached by taking routes 63 and then 66, the Melvin H. Evans Highway which runs east along the south coast.

Our route continues along Centerline Road. Shortly after passing the junction with route 64 on the right, you reach the access road to **St. George Village** and the **St. George Botanical Garden** (☎ 772-3824), one of the island's major attractions. The gardens and woodlands cover about 16 acres (6 hectares) and are laid out around the ruins of the nineteenth century St. George Village, where you can still see the old cottages, blacksmith's forge, watermill, lime kilns and the cemetery. It is thought that there might have been an Arawak settlement on the site. The garden with its many trails, boasts more than a 1,000 species of plants, which represent all the different vegetation belts to be found on the island. The gardens are open daily from 8.30am to 3pm and guided tours are available to learn more about the many plants, most of which have practical uses. There is a small admission charge.

You then rejoin Centerline Road to visit the **Cruzan Rum Distillery** (☎ 772-0799) a small detour back to West Airport Road (route 64). The tour takes in the maturation sheds and the distillery with its wonderful aromas and fumes, past the bottling line to the tasting room, where preferred samples can be bought. It is open daily 8.30am to 4.15pm, and admission is free.

Route 64 heads south to the Alexander Hamilton International Airport which is on the left, and Flamboyant Racetrack on the right. The Melvyn H. Evans Highway (route 64) then heads north past the 130 acre (52 hectare) St. Croix campus of the College of the Virgin Island.

To the south is the **Container Port** and **Port Hess**. Most of the island's industry is concentrated in this area with the massive Amerada-Hess oil refinery, and the nearby alumina works, built at a cost of $25 million, and closed down after little more than 10 years. Although it has now re-opened, production is largely determined by demand and the plant shuts down when world prices are low.

Turn left on to route 79 at the Sunny Isle for the **Island Center**, which is on the journey north back into Christiansted. This is the island's cultural heart. There is a 600-seat theater and open-air 1,600-seat amphitheater, and the Center attracts performers and groups from around the world, as well as providing a platform for many of the island's most talented artists. Nearby is the island's hospital, and to the east on Centerline Road, the old Danish School, which was built in 1840. You can take either routes 74 or 75 west from route 79 to get back to Christiansted.

## EATING OUT ON THE WESTERN TOUR

| Inexpensive | $ |
| Moderate | $$ |
| Expensive | $$$ |

**Biondi's Cafe** $-$$ Frederiksted, Old Town Mall, Italian and deli ☎ 772-4848

**Blue Moon** $-$$ Frederiksted, lively Creole ☎ 772-2222

**Cafe du Soleil** $$-$$$ Frederiksted, Prince Passage, Continental ☎ 772-5400

**Carambola Beach Resort** — Mahogany Room Restaurant $$-$$$ Davis Bay, West Indian and international, Saman Room $-$$ American and seafood ☎ 778-3800. Great Sunday brunch.

**Crocodile** $ Frederiksted, Royal Dane Hotel, French ☎ 772-5700

**Hideway** $$-$$$ Hibiscus Beach, International and Creole ☎ 773-4042

*Following pages: The Anglican Church at Frederiksted, St Croix*

**La Grange Beach Club** $-$$
sandwiches, burgers, fast food
☎ 772-0100

**Le St. Tropez** $$ Frederiksted, Limetree Court, King Street, French bistro ☎ 772-3000

**Motown Bar and Restaurant** $$ Frederiksted Harbor, Seafood, Creole and Continental
☎ 772-9882

**On the Beach Bar and Cafe** $-$$
Frederiksted ☎ 772-4242

**St. Croix By The Sea Restaurant** $$-$$$ Excellent seafood
☎ 778-8600

**Pier 69** $$ Frederiksted, King Street, American and West Indian ☎ 772-0069. Nightly entertainment.

**Sprat Hall Restaurant** $$$ Sprat Hall Beach, Seafood and Creole
☎ 772-0305

**Tradewinds Deli** $-$$
Tradewinds Mall, Hot and cold sandwiches ☎ 772-0718

**Vel's Bar and Restaurant** $-$$
Frederiksted, King Street, Latin cuisine and seafood. Excellent conch dishes ☎ 772-2160.

**Villa Morales** $$ Frederiksted, Creole and Island specialities
☎ 772-0556

## THE EASTERN TOUR

Head east along the coast from Christiansted on route 82 which is also East End Road. Fort St. Jean, named when the French controlled the island, was renamed **Batteriet Louise Augusta** during Danish times.

**Altona Lagoon** has a fine public beach with changing facilities and rest rooms, and as it is just east of Christiansted, it is popular with the islanders at weekends. It is part of **Gallows Bay** and near the Fort Louise Augusta radio tower. Gallows Bay was the main port of St. Croix until the 1960s and the marina played host to the yachts and small cruise ships visiting the island.

Follow East End Road with Seven Hills and Mount Washington 527ft (161m) to the south. It passes the private **Buccaneer Beach**, accessible for a small charge, and the luxury Buccaneer resort with its championship 18-hole golf course, and eight championship Laykold surface tennis courts overlooking Cutlass Cove Beach. It is set in 200 acres (80 hectares) of tropical gardens with many of the trees and plants labelled for identification. The first buildings on the Buccaneer Estate were constructed in 1653 by Charles Martel, a Knight of Malta, and were built out of sight of the sea to protect it from roving pirates. It was later the home of Danish Governor von Prock and Alexander Hamilton, then a sugar mill plantation and cattle ranch before becoming a hotel. It has been owned by the Armstrong family since 1922 and the Armstrongs have been on St. Croix for nine generations.

**Shoy Beach** at **Punnett Point**, is accessed by a rough road past the golf course and then a path down to the beach. Offshore is Green Cay with its marina and National Wildlife Refuge. The island has many herons and pelicans and is a sanctuary for the St. Croix ground lizard. It is possible to take a boat trip out to the island which offers an excellent view of the teeming bird life on the cliffs. Green Cay Marina is on the mainland and attracts yachts from around the world.

Drive past **Chenay Bay** and the **Chenay Bay Beach Resort**, and **Coakley Bay** and **Solitude Bay** to **Tague Bay** and the **Reef golf course** and the **St. Croix Yacht Club**, and inland is Cotton Valley.

About 1½ miles (2km) off the coast to the north is the 880 acre (352 hectare) **Buck Island Reef National Monument**, which takes in the 180 acre (72 hectare) island and the rest is the surrounding turquoise sea. It is a fascinating underwater marine park with clear warm waters and coral reefs. Buck Island lies off Solitude Bay on the north-eastern side of St. Croix, and was declared a National Monument because of the barrier coral reef that lies of its eastern coast. Danish settlers who moved in the mid-eighteenth century called it Pocken-Ey Land (Germanic for the lignum vitae, which grew everywhere). It was later changed to 'Buck' because of a typographical error on a map. Sailors would leave goats on small islands like this so that they would have supplies of fresh meat next time they passed. Unfortunately, the goats thrived and almost ate the island bare before they were rounded up and removed in the 1950s. Since then and under careful management and planting, the island has been allowed to return to its near natural former state, and now attracts many species of birds and butterflies. There are more than 60 species of trees, and the island, which rises to 340ft (104m) above sea level, is home to many brown pelicans, the threatened Least Tern and frigate birds, and three species of endangered turtles — green, leatherback and hawksbill. The reef is what most people come to see, however, and it has many species of coral, including staghorn, elkhorn and brain coral, and is host to teeming shoals of brightly-coloured tropical fish. The waters are

exceptionally clear and shallow, rarely more than 12ft (4m) deep, and a trail has been marked out which can easily be followed using only snorkel and mask. There are several species of coral among the reefs which are home to about 90 species of fish. Most of the reef consists of elkhorn coral, and this together with the protected lagoon comprise the Marine Garden. There are frequent boat trips and tours from Christiansted to Buck Island, and access to the island is permitted between sunrise and sunset. It makes a great day out and there is a fine sandy beach with picnic tables and barbecue pits provided, observation platform and pretty hiking trail which takes a leisurely 45 minutes.

To the right inland is **Fairleigh Dickinson University's West Indies Laboratory** for marine studies. As you travel eastwards, the vegetation changes

*Grape Tree Bay, St Croix*

dramatically because of the lower rainfall, and there are lots of cactus and scrub plants. Many trees along this North Shore Road had their crowns snapped off in the hurricane and were literally blasted smooth by flying salt so that they now resemble modern sculptures. There is a restaurant at Reef Beach and because of the winds round the headland, it is a popular spot with windsurfers. Nearby is the Reef golf course, and the West Indies Laboratory, established in 1971 by Fairleigh Dickinson University of New Jersey, to study the island geography, biology and marine life. They also operate a hydrolab in Salt Bay.

Past Cottongarden Point you can take the unpaved but passable road to **Point Udall**, also known as East Point, the most easterly point on the island, and the most easterly point of land under the US flag. The road (route 82) is paved as far as the beach and tidal pool area. During the winter, the St. Croix Environmental Society conduct historic nature hikes in the area ☎ 773-1989. Do not try to drive down tracks to get to beaches without checking them out first. It is usually better to park at the top and walk down.

There are fine views of Buck Island from Cottongarden Point. To the east is the **Cramer Recreation Park** with rest rooms and changing facilities. There is a lovely beach and a bar and restaurant which specialises in island cooking.

You cannot miss the massive 82ft (25m) diameter antenna, which was built by the National Science Foundation at a cost of $5 million. The dish 1 mile (2km) from the point, is operated by the National Radio Astronomy Observatory, and weighs 260 tons. It is one of ten being used to explore the outer reaches of the universe. It is part of a network of similar antennae dotted through the United States which together form one massive radio telescope. There are free tours of the site which is usually open daily.

Return along the unpaved road and then take route 60 south for **Isaac Point** which protects Isaac's Bay and is usually quiet. The waters offer excellent snorkelling. As you drive south and then west, you will notice the vegetation starting to become richer again.

The route passes by Jack Bay to the east and the road then heads west along the South Shore Road to Grapetree Point and the Divi Resort, destroyed in Hurricane Hugo. The beautiful **Grapetree Beach** stretches for several hundred yards and has facilities for eating and water sports. Up on the hills you can see the striking Contessa's Castle, a private residence that always seems to be having more bits added on. Owned by Contessa Nadia Faber it looks like two castles built around the Taj Mahal, and it has stunning 360 degree views perched as it is atop the hill.

Continue to Turner Hole, Grassy Point, Red Bay ,Robin Bay, Seven Mile Reef to **Great Salt Pond Bay** with its coral reef. Nearby are the ruins of **Estate Great Pond** and Camp Arawak, and there is a nature trail providing great birdwatching. The South Shore Road (route 60) runs inland round Great Salt Pond, and then north. Turn left on to route

624 and then left again by the filling station, on to route 62 which is Southside Road. (If you turn right on to Lowry Hill Road, route 62, it is only a short drive north-west back into Christiansted).

After Spring Bay there is **Manchenil Bay** with its fine sand beach and **Canegarden Bay** is an interesting area. Apart from the beach this is an area of salt flats and ponds, a haven for birdlife. There are also many trails in the area to be explored. The vegetaion is stunted and sparse because of the much hotter temperatures than elsewhere on the island.

The route inland back to Christiansted is through very agricultural land and you pass the Dairies, which provide the island with fresh milk and other dairy products. The red cattle are Senepols, specially bred on St. Croix. They are a cross breed between the traditional English Red Poll and the much larger drought-tolerant Senegal from Africa. There are also many signs of the area's long agricultural history with the ruins of eighteenth- and nineteenth-century sugar mills.

You can then either take route 83 or connect with route 70, the Queen Mary Highway, north back into Chistiansted, the last stretch of this road is aptly named Contentment Road.

## EATING OUT ON THE EASTERN TOUR

| Inexpensive | $ |
| Moderate | $$ |
| Expensive | $$$ |

**Baggy Wrinkle** $ American Gallows Bay ☎ 773-4402

**Brass Parrot** $$$ East End, Buccaneer Hotel, West Indian and Continental ☎ 773-2100

**Chenay Bay** $$ Green Cay, West Indian and American ☎ 773-2918

**Cultured Pelican Restaurants** $$ Coakley Bay, Italian ☎ 773-3333

**Duggan's Reef** $$ Teague Bay, Seafood and international ☎ 773-9800

**Galleon** $$ Green Cay, Continental and seafood ☎ 773-9949

**Harbormaster Beach Club** $$ Hotel on the Cay, relaxed American and Creole, entertainment ☎ 773-2035

**No Bones Cafe** $-$$ Gallows Bay, Seafood and grills ☎ 773-2128

**Spinnakers Grill** $-$$ Gallows Bay, Seafood, steaks and fast food ☎ 773-3800

# Traveller's Tips

| | | | |
|---|---|---|---|
| Accommodation | 131 | Pharmacies | 146 |
| Hotels – St. Thomas | 131 | Photographs | 146 |
| Apartments & Luxury Villas | | Post | 147 |
| St. Thomas | 134 | Public Holidays & Festivals | 147 |
| Hotels – St. Croix | 134 | Security | 149 |
| Apartments & Villas | | Sports | 149 |
| St. Croix | 137 | Diving | 149 |
| Hotels – St. John | 137 | Fishing | 151 |
| Airlines | 138 | Golf | 152 |
| Banks | 139 | Horse Racing | 152 |
| Beauty Salons | 139 | Horse Riding | 152 |
| Campsites | 139 | Kayaking | 152 |
| Car Hire & Driving Rules | 139 | Power Boats | 152 |
| Rules of the Road | 140 | Surfing | 153 |
| Carnival | 141 | Tennis | 153 |
| Churches | 141 | Water Sports | 153 |
| Cinema-Movies | 141 | Yachts | 153 |
| Clothing & Packing | 142 | Taxes | 154 |
| Currency | 142 | Taxis | 154 |
| Customs & Immigration | 142 | St. Thomas | 154 |
| Disabled | 143 | St. John | 154 |
| Electricity | 143 | St. Croix | 154 |
| Embassies & Consulates | 143 | Telephones | 155 |
| Gambling | 144 | Time | 155 |
| Health | 144 | Tipping | 155 |
| Insurance | 144 | Tourist Offices | 155 |
| Irritating Insects | 145 | Tour Operators | 156 |
| Media | 145 | Water | 157 |
| Nightlife | 146 | Weddings | 157 |
| Pets | 146 | | |

## ACCOMMODATION:

Every conceivable type of accommodation can be found on the islands from luxury resorts to campgrounds in the National Park. There is accommodation to suit all tastes and pockets ranging from large hotels to guest houses, self-catering apartments to private villas, and from efficiency units to camping cabins. Most hotels offer special packages which are much cheaper than normal daily rates, and airlines often offer accommodation packages as well which can mean significant savings. Many hotels also offer special deals for honeymoon couples, and packages for those with particular interests, such as diving, water sports, golf, and even bird watching.

Some hotels will not accept young children, and some are adult only, but most welcome children and offer special packages, and provide special facilities and entertainment for them, such as baby sitting and supervised playgrounds and pool areas.

With such a range of accommodation available, and three islands to choose from, it is important to shop around and make sure you pick the island and accommodation most suited to your needs. If you cannot decide, why not spend some time on each of the islands, as they all have something different to offer. Hotels are price rated as follows: $ - inexpensive, $$ - moderate, $$$ - expensive

### *St. Thomas*
Hotels
**Admirals Inn** $$ Waterfront bed and breakfast inn close to the harbour with pool, and close to shops, restaurants and beach ☎ 774-1376

**Blackbeard's Castle** $$ Hilltop overlooking St. Thomas Harbour with restaurant, bar and pool ☎ 776-1234

**Bluebeard's Castle** $$$ Luxury hilltop resort with restaurants, bars, shops, tennis and pool. Honeymoon and tennis packages available ☎ 774-1600

**Bolongo Club Everything Beach Resort** $$-$$$ 78 rooms and family villas, luxury beachfront resort with three restaurants, bars, pool, tennis, luxury yachts, kiddies beach club and headquarters of the St. Thomas diving school offering full instruction, equipment hire and dive trips. All-inclusive packages are available ☎ 775-1800

**Bolongo Elysian** $$-$$$ Cowpet Bay, lively beachside resort with restaurant, bar, pool, fitness center and health spa, and nightly live entertainment. ☎ 1-800-524-4746

**Bunker Hill Hotel** $-$$ Charlotte Amalie, Comfortable bed and breakfast with pool, Commandant Gade ☎ 774-8056

**Carib Beach Resort** $$ secluded beachside accommodation with restaurant, bar, watersports, diving ☎ 774-2525

**Danish Chalet Inn** $$ Charlotte Amalie,13 very comfortable rooms ☎ 774-5764

**Embers Guest House** $ inland from Crown Bar, close to beaches and shops ☎ 777-8131

**Emerald Beach Resort** $$-$$$ Luxury beachfront setting, restaurant, bar, watersports ☎ 777-8800

**Frenchman's Reef** $$$ Ultra-luxurious beachfront resort complex including the 518-room Frenchman's Reef and neighbouring 96-room Morningstar Beach Club. Seven restaurants, bars, Olympic size pools, tennis, shops, waterside taxis to town, snorkelling, diving, sea fishing and nightly entertainment ☎ 776-8500

**Galleon House** $ On Government Hill. A comfortable bed and breakfast hotel with pool ☎ 774-6952

**Grand Palazzo** $$$ Great Bay. Luxury suites overlook the mangroves and beach, with three restaurants, bars, pool, watersports, sailing and boat trips, snorkelling-dive center, tennis, shops, beaty salon and fitness center, and nightly entertainment. The resort also has conference facilities. Nearby golf ☎ 775-3333

**Harbor View** $-$$ An early eighteenth century French manor house with small dining room and pool ☎ 774-2651

**Hotel 1829** $$$ A lovely inn on Government Hill and a National Historic Site. Noted for its restaurant, with bar, pool and charming gardens ☎ 776-1829

**Island Beachcomber** $$ 50 room beachside hotel at Lindbergh Bay. Outdoor garden restaurant, snorkelling and water rafts ☎ 774-5250

**Le Petit Motel** $ Close to downtown Charlotte Amalie ☎ 775-2310

**Limetree Beach** $$$ 84 rooms. A secluded all-inclusive luxury hotel popular with honeymooners. Excellent restaurants, bars, pool, tennis, scuba instruction, sailing. Entertainment most nights. Wednesday night is Carnival night. Noted for its near-tame iguanas who join you for dinner ☎ 776-4770

**Magens Point Hotel** $$ On Magens Bay Road with restaurant, bar, and pool, and close to the beach and golf ☎ 775-5500

**Point Pleasant** $$$ Overlooking Smith Bay, with restaurants, bars, tennis, snorkelling, sailing, complimentary use of hotel cars ☎ 775-7200

**The Mark St.Thomas** $$$ A delightful eighteenth century former Great House and now an elegant small hotel with delightful rooms, restaurant, piano bar and pool ☎ 774-5511

**Miller Manor** $ Charlotte Amalie, Friendly small guest house ☎ 774-1535

**Morning Star Beach Resort** $$$ Sister property of Frenchman's Reef (see above)

**Pavilions and Pools** $$$ Luxury units each with their own pool, with restaurant, pool and water sports ☎ 775-6110

**Ramada Yacht Haven** $$-$$$ Large, comfortable hotel overlooking the harbour with restaurants, bars and pool, and conference facilities ☎ 774-9700

**Point Pleasant Resort** $$-$$$ Water Bay, set in woodlands and gardens overlooking the sea. Ideal for honeymooners ☎ 775-7200 or 1-800-524-2300

**Sapphire Beach Resort and Marina** $$$ Beachfront villas and suites, with restaurant, waterside bar, marina, tennis, water sports and nightly entertainment ☎ 775-6100

**Secret Harbour** $$-$$$ 60 secluded luxury beachfront suites on delightful Nazareth Bay, with candlelit oceanside terrace restaurant, tennis, sailing, hiking, deep sea fishing, diving and watersports, and nearby golf. Popular with honeymooners ☎ 775-6550

**Stouffer Renaissance Grand Beach** $$$ Luxury beachfront resort close to Coral World, with noted gourmet restaurant, bars, disco, pools, tennis and watersports ☎ 775-1510

**Villa Blanca** $$ 12 rooms on Estate Tutu ☎ 776-0749

**West Indies Inn** $-$$ In Frenchtown. Very comfortable small hotel offering breakfast and close to many restaurants for other meals ☎ 774-1376

**Windward Passage** $$ 146 rooms. Downtown and overlooking the harbour with courtyard restaurant, bar and pool ☎ 774-5200

**Wyndham Sugar Bay Plantation Resort** $$-$$$ Sugar Bay, luxury resort with restaurant, bar, waterpark with three pools, whirlpool, beach, tennis, snorkelling, fitness center, watersports, boat trips. It also has extensive conference facilities, large ballroom, and 112-seat amphitheatre ☎ 1-800-927-7100

<u>Apartments and Luxury Villas</u>
**Anchorage Beach Villas** $-$$ 30 units on route 6, with tennis, pool and watersports ☎ 775-6220.

**Blazing Villas** $$ Tennis, health club ☎ 716-3600

**Cowpet Bay Villas** $-$$ 25 units close to the beach on Nazareth Bay, with restaurant, pool, tennis and jacuzzi ☎ 775-6000

**Red Hook Mountain Apartments** $-$$ 10 units with fabulous views ☎ 775-6111.

**Sea Horses Cottages** $-$$ 25 cottages overlooking St. John and the beach ☎ 775-9231

**Watergate Villas** $$ 140 units on Estate Bolongo with pools, tennis and watersports

### St. Croix

Almost all the properties had to be rebuilt after Hurricane Hugo, and now offer high standards, both in terms of buildings and facilities offered.

<u>Hotels</u>
**Anchor Inn** $$ 31 rooms, King St. Christiansted. On the waterfront downtown with restaurant, bar, pool and water sports ☎ 773-4000.

**Best Western Holger Danske** $-$$ King Cross Street, Christiansted ☎ 773-3600

**The Buccanneer** $$$ 150 rooms, Gallows Bay. Luxury resort on 300 acre (120 hectare) estate dating back to 1647, with four noted restaurants, bars, pools, beaches, watersports, tennis, golf, horseback riding, health spa, kiddies club, jogging and nature trails and arcade. It also has conference facilities, wedding

## TRAVELLER'S TIPS

and honeymoon packages
☎ 773-2100 or 1-800-223-1108

**Cane Bay Reef Club** $$ 9 suites, Cane Bay Beach. Restaurant, pool, diving, watersports, golf nearby ☎ 778-2966.

**Carambola Beach Resort** $$$ 151 rooms, Davis Bay. Luxury beachfront hotel with three restaurants, bars, pool, watersports, shops, deli, library, meeting rooms, health club, floodlit tennis and championship golf course ☎ 778-3800 or 1-800-333-3333

**Caravelle Hotel** $$ 44 rooms, Queen Cross Street, Christiansted. Award winning hotel overlooking the harbour with waterside restaurant, pool, diving shop. Honeymoon packages
☎ 773-0687 or 1-800-524-0410

**Chenay Bay Beach Resort** $$ 50 rooms, Chenay Bay. Beachfront cottage resort, with beachfront restaurant, pool, tennis, snorkelling, kayaks, windsurfing school and shuttle to town. Regular evening entertainment ☎ 773-2918 or 1-800-548-4457

**Club Comanche** $-$$ 42 rooms, Strand Street, Christiansted. Part of the downtown building dates from the 1750s ☎ 773-0210.

**Cormorant Beach Club** $$$ 38 rooms, La Grande Princess. Luxury beach front villas and rooms, with all-day restaurant, bar, pool, beach, tennis, snorkelling, watersports and croquet ☎ 778-8920 or 1-800-548-4460

**Danish Manor Hotel** $-$$ Company Street, Christiansted. A charming, comfortable bed and breakfast establishment with delightful Danish courtyard, bar and pool ☎ 773-1377

**Hotel on the Cay** $$$ on Protestant Cay and a 2 minute ferry trip from Christiansted. Restaurant, bar, pool, beaches, watersports ☎ 773-2035

**Frederiksted** $-$$ 40 rooms in town overlooking the harbour with pool and frequent nightly entertainment ☎ 772-0500

**Hibiscus Beach Hotel** $$ 37 rooms, La Grande Princesse. Beachside Caribbean-style hotel with restaurant, bar, pool and watersports ☎ 773-4042 or 1-800-442-0121

**Hilty House Inn** $$ 6 rooms, close to Christiansted. Elegant plantation inn in tropical gardens, with pool. ☎ 773-2594

**Hotel on the Cay** $$-$$$ exclusive beach resort on inland in Christiansted harbour with restaurant, bar, and wide range of watersports ☎ 773-2035 or 1-800-773-2035

**King Christian Hotel** $-$$ waterfront Christiansted with pool and dockside restaurant, close to beach, tennis, golf, watersports ☎ 773-2285

**King Frederik** $-$$ 39 rooms, small beachside hotel just outside Frederiksted, with patio dining, bar and pool ☎ 772-1205

**King's Alley** $$ Christiansted. Restaurant, bar and pool ☎ 773-0103.

**Kronegade Inn** $-$$ beach club, Western Suburb, Christiansted ☎ 692-9590

**Moonraker** $-$$ Queen Cross Street, Christiansted. Downtown small comfortable hotel, with lively evening lounge ☎ 773-1535.

**On The Beach Resort** $-$$ beachside restaurant, bar and pool, Frederiksted ☎ 772-1205

**Pink Fancy** $$ 13 rooms, Prince Street, Chistiansted. Comfortable and friendly rooms in town house with breakfast ☎ 773-8460

**Royal Dane** $ Strand Street, Frederiksted. By the harbour with French restaurant ☎ 772-2780.

**St. Croix By The Sea** $$$ 65 rooms. A luxury oceanfront hotel with three restaurants, bar, boutique, watersports and the largest saltwater pool in the Caribbean. There are also conference facilities ☎ 778-8600 or 1-800-524-5006

**Schooner Bay** $$ Christiansted. Harbourside resort overlooking the bay with pool, tennis, adjacent restaurant and shops ☎ 1-800-524-2025

**Sprat Hall** $$ 16 rooms, a former Plantation Great House built in the mid-seventeenth century, with two restaurants, pool, beach, horseback riding, fishing, diving and water sports ☎ 772-0305.

**Tamarind Reef Hotel** $$ 46 rooms, Green Cay Marina. Oceanfront rooms overlooking coral reef, with restaurant, snack bar and bar, watersports, diving and sailing ☎ 773-4455 or 1-800-619-0014

**Waves at Cane Bay** $-$$ 12 rooms

on the beach with watersports and diving and close to golf ☎ 778-1805 or 1-800-545-0603

<u>Apartments and Villas</u>
There are many apartments on the island. These include:

**Antilles at Colony Cove** $$
☎ 773-9150

**Carden Beach** $$-$$$ coastal locations overlooking Buck Island ☎ 773-9333

**Caribbean View** $$ La Grande Princess ☎ 773-3335

**Club St. Croix** $$$ Estate Golden Rock ☎ 773-4800

**Colony Cove Resorts** $$ Estate Golden Rock. Beachfront suite resort, with pool, tennis, watersports and herb and tea gardens ☎ 773-1965 or 1-800-828-0746

**Cormorant Beach Club** $$$ Cormorant Beach ☎ 778-8920

**Estate Tipperary** $$$ Luxury private villa ☎ (508) 692-8813

**Gentel Winds Resorts** $$
☎ 778-3400

**Long Reef Condominium** $$ Just west of Christiansted, set in tropical gardens with pool and close to restaurants, golf, shops ☎ 1-800-524-2025

**Mill Harbour** $$ Estate Golden Rock ☎ 524-2008

**Sugar Beach Resort** $$ Estate Golden Rock ☎ 524-2049

**Villa Madelaine** $$$ On the hills overlooking Gallows Bay with open air restaurant, bar and magnificent views. All villas have their own pools ☎ 773-8141

Villa rentals can be arranged through Island Villas ☎ 773-8821, Teague Bay Properties ☎ 1-800-237-1959, and Tropic Retreats in Paradise ☎ 778-7550.

### *St. John*
<u>Hotels</u>

**Caneel Bay** $$$ Deluxe resort set in tropical gardens along seven superb beaches. There are three restaurants, the excellent Equator Restaurant in an eighteenth-century sugar mill, bars, tennis, boat cruises, sailing, scuba, snorkelling, inshore fishing, parasailing, aerobics, golf, walking and watersports. It also has conference facilities. It has its own dock and ferry service running between the resort and Charlotte

Amalia on St. Thomas
☎ 776-6111.

**Cruz Inn** $ a comfortable bed and breakfast guesthouse close to town, with bar
☎ 776-7688.

**Estate Concordia** $$ Cruz Bay, secluded units ☎ 693-5855

**Gallows Point** $$-$$$ on the cliffs just outside Cruz Bay, with restaurant and stunning views
☎ 776-6434

**Harmony** $$-$$$ Great Salt Pond, Eco-tourist resort with beach, restaurant, bar, watersports
☎ 776-6240

**Inn at Tamarind Court** $-$$ In Cruz Bay and offering good value
☎ 776-6378

**Hyatt Regency St. John** $$$ Great Cruz Bay, luxury resort with two restaurants, bars, pool, tennis, ballroom, watersports, luxury yacht ferry service and conference facilities ☎ 776-7171 or 1-800-223-1234

**Intimate Inn** $$$ Overlooking Cruz bay ☎ 776-6133

**Lavender Hill Estates** $$ luxury condos, Cruz Bay ☎ 776-6969

**Raintree Inn** $-$$ Close to the harbour, with restaurant
☎ 776-7449.

**Villa Bougainvillea** $$ Luxury condos ☎ 776-6420

**Virgin Grand Villas** $$-$$$
☎ 693-8977

There are a large number of apartments, villas and cottages on the island, and a number of private homes are also available for rental. Contacts include: Holiday Homes ☎ 776-6776, Private Homes for Private Vacations ☎ 776-6876, St. John Properties ☎ 776-7223, Vacation Vistas ☎ 776-6462, Vacation Homes ☎ 776-6519, and Vacation Retreats ☎ 776-7001.

## AIRLINES
**Air Anguilla** ☎ 776-5789
**American Airline**
☎ 1-800-433-7300
**American Eagle** ☎ 774-6464
or 1-800-474-4884
**Bohlke International Airways**
☎ 778-9177
**British Airways**
☎ 1-800-247-9297
**BWIA** ☎ 1-800-327-7401
**Continental** ☎ 777-8199 or
1-800-231-0856
**Delta** ☎ 777-4177
or 1-800-221-1212

**Iberia** ☎ 1-800-772-4642
**LIAT** ☎ 774-2313
**Lufthansa** ☎ 1-800-645-3880
**Northwest** ☎ 1-800-225-2525
**TWA** ☎ 1-800-892-4141
**US Air** ☎ 774-7885
   or 1-800-842-5374
**United** ☎ 1-800-538-2929
**Windward Island Airways**
   ☎ 775-0183

## BANKS

Banks are generally open Monday to Thursday from 9am to 2.30pm and from 9am to 2pm, and 3.30pm to 5pm on Friday. Banks are not open at weekends or on public holidays.

## BEAUTY SALONS

There are many beauty salons on the islands both in town and at most of the large hotels and resorts.

## CAMPSITES

There is limited private camping on St. Croix, at Cramer Park, Camp Arawak, near Christiansted, and Estate Fareham, near Greatpond. Facilities are limited and there may not be fresh water. There are two good campsites within the boundaries of the St. John National Park. Cinnamon Bay offers bare pitches, cottages and erected tents. Cottages and erected tents are equipped with lights, stove, table and chairs, ice chest, cooking utensils, beds and bed linen. There are communal toilets and showers, and a café and small shop. Other facilities include snorkelling, diving, watersports and day sailing. There are evening presentations in the amphitheater about environmental and natural history issues. The campground is very popular and reservations are strongly recommended. Stays are limited to a maximum of 2 weeks. Contact: Cinnamon Bay Camp, Box 720, St. John United States Virgin Island 00830 ☎ 776-6330. The privately-run Maho Bay offers 105 tent cottages sleeping four adults, with restaurant, shop and bathhouse on site. Contact: Maho Bay Camp, Cruz Bay, St. John, United States Virgin Islands 00830 ☎ 776-6226.

## CAR HIRE AND DRIVING RULES

Hire cars are readily available. DRIVING IS ON THE LEFT HAND SIDE OF THE ROAD — British style and a carry over from Danish rule — although most vehicles have

US style steering wheels on the left rather than the right. A valid US driving licence allows you to drive a hire car for up to 90 days provided you are aged 18 or over. Non US citizens with a valid licence need to get a temporary licence, which are available from the car rental companies. If you are staying longer than 90 days, you must get a USVI licence. Main roads are well signposted and most island maps refer to them both by name and number.

Road conditions vary enormously and range from generally very good in main towns to very difficult in remote areas, especially on St. John. The locals tend to drive fast so caution needs to be exercised, especially on narrow roads and blind corners. Parking in the main towns can also pose a problem, especially when a cruise ship is in port. Scooters and motor bikes are available to anyone aged 15 and over.

Car hire is available from around $40-45 a day for unlimited mileage, and four-wheel drive vehicles are preferable if you want to explore the islands fully.

**Rules of the road:** Drive on the left, look out for one-way streets, there are no right turns when lights are red, but left turns at red lights are allowed if the road is clear. Sound your horn when approaching blind corners, and always be alert. Many local drivers brake rapidly to pick up or drop off friends.

Main car hire companies include:

**ABC Rentals**, St. Thomas ☎ 776-1222
**A Better Rental**, St. Thomas ☎ 777-8888
**Aristocrat Car Rental**, St. Thomas ☎ 776-0026
**Atlas Car Rentals**, St. Croix ☎ 773-2886
**Avis,** St. Croix ☎ 778-9365, St. John ☎ 776-6375, St. Thomas ☎ 774-4616
**Budget,** St. Croix ☎ 778-9636, St Thomas ☎ 776-5774
**C and C Car and Jeep Rental**, Cruz Bay, St. John ☎ 693-8164
**Caribbean Jeep and Car**, St. Croix ☎ 778-1000, St. Thomas ☎ 776-4399
**Cool Breeze Rental**, St. John ☎ 776-6588
**Cowpet Car Rental**, St. Thomas ☎ 775-7376
**Dependable**, St. Thomas ☎ 777-9535
**Discount** St. Thomas ☎ 776-4858
**Dollar**, St. Thomas ☎ 776-1977
**E-Z Car Rentals**, St. Thomas ☎ 775-6255
**Green Cay Jeep and Car Rental,** ☎ 773-7227

**Hertz**, St. Croix ☎ 778-1402, St. Thomas ☎ 774-1879
**Hospitality Rent-a-Car**, Cruz Bay, St. John ☎ 693-9160
**National Car Rental**, St. Thomas ☎ 776-3616
**Paradise**, St. Thomas ☎ 776-5335
**Preferred Rentals**, St. Croix ☎ 778-1402
**Sea Breeze**, St. Thomas ☎ 774-7200
**Spencer's Jeep Rental**, St. John ☎ 693-8784
**St. Croix Jeep and Honda Rentals** ☎ 773-0161
**Sun Island**, St. Thomas ☎ 774-3333
**Thrifty**, St. Croix ☎ 773-7200
**VI Auto Rental**, St. Thomas ☎ 776-3616

Scooters can be rented on St. Croix from Island Scooters ☎ 778-7470, American Scooter Rental ☎ 773-3278, and R.C. Scooter Rentals ☎ 778-8822.

## CARNIVAL

St. Thomas — after Easter
St. John — first week of July

## CHURCHES

The following denominations are represented

**St. Croix** — Apostolic, Baptist, Christian Scientist, Church of God, Episcopalian, Hindu, Jehovah's Witness, Jewish, Lutheran, Methodist, Moravian, Moslem, Presbyterian, Roman Catholic, Salvation Army and Seventh Day Adventist.

**St. John** — Baptist, Christian Scientist, Episcopalian, Jehovah's Witness, Lutheran, Methodist, Moravian, Presbyterian, Roman Catholic and Seventh Day Adventist.

**St. Thomas** — Apostolic, Baha'i, Baptist, Christian Scientist, Episcopalian, Hindu, Jehovah's Witness, Jewish, Lutheran, Methodist, Moravian, Moslem, Presbyterian, Roman Catholic, Salvation Army and Seventh Day Adventist.

## CINEMA-MOVIES

There are several movie theaters on St. Thomas and St. Croix showing the latest releases, while on St. John, films are usually screened in local bars.

## CLOTHING AND PACKING

Light, loose and informal clothing is best. Swimwear is fine on the beach or by the pool, but cover up a little if walking around town or going for a meal. Most hotels and restaurants do not have dress codes, although some prefer men to wear jackets but not ties, for dinner. Many people, however, after spending a day on the beach like to dress up for dinner and there are no problems if you want to do this.

Evening temperatures can dip just a little, and a sweater, light jacket or wrap can come in useful. Pack sandals for the beach as the sand can get too hot to walk on, and if you plan to go walking in the interior, take lightweight trousers and sturdy footwear. A lightweight waterproof jacket is also a good idea if you plan to go hiking, sailing or similar.

A hat, sunglasses and a good sunscreen lotion are also essential, and if you do not have a sun hat, buy a straw hat as soon as you arrive on the islands because they are perfect for the job and make great souvenirs.

It is also a good idea to pack a good insect repellant, shampoos and any prescribed medications.

## CURRENCY

The currency is the US dollar but travellers cheques and major credit cards are accepted at most hotels, restaurants and large shops. It is a good idea to keep several $1 bills for tips and so on, and not a good idea to carry large denomination notes such as $50 and $100, as many shops will be reluctant or unable to change them. Most establishments will not accept private cheques.

## CUSTOMS AND IMMIGRATION

Visitors from UK and mainland Europe require a full passport (a British Visitor's Passport will not be accepted). You do not have to have a visa if your stay is for less than 90 days, but you must fill in a visa waiver form which you will be given by the airline at check-in or on board the plane. This form must be handed to the immigration officer on arrival. If you plan to interrupt your journey by flying on to another Caribbean island or to the US mainland, or are on business, a visa is advisable, and can be obtained by mail from the United States Embassy in your country. You must have a valid return ticket and may be required to show it.

Visitors from the United States and Canada must have some proof of citizenship, such as birth certificate, voter's registration card or passport. If you plan to take a day trip to one of the British Virgin Islands, a passport will be needed.

No vaccinations are required.

Because of the free port status of the islands, visitors returning to the US can take back up to $1,200 worth of duty-free goods, and there is a flat rate tax of 5 per cent on the next $1,000 of purchases above this allowance. The allowance also includes five cartons of cigarettes, and if over the age of 21, up to 1 gallon (5 litres) of spirits or alcohol, provided one bottle is a local product i.e. an island rum, otherwise the allowance is five 75cc bottles. There is no limit on goods bought and made on the islands, although all receipts and certificates of origin, provided by the retailer, must be kept for inspection if required. You can mail an unlimited number of gifts back to the US as long as each is worth $100 or less.

Canadian Custom regulations are tougher, and returning visitors are only allowed Canadian $300 worth of duty free goods, provided they have not claimed any exemptions in the previous 12 months.

## DISABLED

Almost all airlines offer assistance to wheelchair and other disabled travellers, and most hotels and resorts will endeavour to provide suitable accommodation — such as rooms on the ground floor — if given advance notice. All the newer hotels have facilities for the disabled, such as ramps and Braille numbers in elevators — but access to the beach, pool, eating areas may be restricted or difficult elsewhere. Always check before making bookings. Further information can be obtained from the VI Commission on the Handicapped.

## ELECTRICITY

The electric supply is 120 volts, 60 cycles alternating current, the same as in the US Adapters are needed for appliances from Europe.

## EMBASSIES AND CONSULATES

Emergency Numbers
Police ☎ 915
Fire ☎ 921
Ambulance 922
Coastguard: St. Thomas ☎ 774-1911, St. Croix ☎ 773-6303
National Park Service ☎ 773-1460

## GAMBLING

St. Croix has sanctioned gambling on the island and a number of resorts featuring casinos are expected to be built over the next few years.

## HEALTH

There are no serious health problems although visitors should take precautions against the sun and biting insects such as sand flies and mosquitoes, both of which can ruin your holiday. Biting bugs tend to come out late in the afternoon. Other minor problem areas include one or two nasty species of wasps, and there are scorpions although these are very rare, and their sting is usually painful rather than dangerous. Be careful around coral and be alert for jelly fish and spiny sea urchins which are occasionally a problem at some times of the year.

Immunisation is not required unless travelling from an infected area.

All the islands have US qualified doctors and dentists and there are modern hospitals providing the full range of care. The St. Thomas Hospital and Community Health Center is on Sugar Estate Road, in Charlotte Amalie, and there are also the St. Thomas Medical Arts Complex, the Walk-In Medical Center, and the Doctors on Call Center.

In St. Croix there is the Governor Juan F. Luis Hospital and Community Health Center, west of Christiansted close to Island Center, the Sunny Isle and Beeston Hill Medical Center, and the smaller Ingeborg Nesbitt Clinic in Frederiksted.

In St. John, the Myrah Keating-Smith Community Health Center in Susannaberg, provides emergency treatment with patients transferred to St. Thomas by ambulance boat or helicopter if necessary.

Most hotels and resorts have doctors on call around the clock, and emergency dental treatment is also available at all times.

Island pharmacies will make up valid prescriptions from mainland US doctors, but visitors from Europe are recommended to bring in prescribed medicines together with a covering letter from your doctor, in case they are not available on the island.

## INSURANCE

Make sure you have adequate insurance to cover all eventualities. Health care if required, is expensive, and if hiring a car, it is worth taking out extra insurance such as damage collision waiver. If you have hired a car as part of a package deal, check what insurance cover this includes, and make up any shortcomings.

## IRRITATING INSECTS

Mosquitoes can be a problem almost anywhere. In your room, burn mosquito coils or use one of the many electrical plug in devices which burn an insect repelling tablet. Mosquitoes are not so much of a problem on or near the beaches because of onshore winds, but they may well bite you as you enjoy an open air evening meal. Use a good insect repellant, especially if you are planning trips inland such as walking in the rain forests. Fire ants are also found in wooded areas, and their bites can be very irritating. Bay rum essences can be soothing.

Lemon grass can be found growing naturally, and a handful of this in your room is also a useful mosquito deterrent.

Sand flies can be a problem on the beach. Despite their tiny size they can give you a nasty bite. Ants abound, so make sure you check the ground carefully before sitting down otherwise you might get bitten, and the bites can itch for days.

## MEDIA

The *Daily News* is published in St. Thomas, and the *St.Croix Avis* is published on St. Croix. Both are published daily except Sunday and on public holidays. Major hotels and news stands also sell US papers such as the *Wall Street Journal* and *USA Today*, which are flown in daily, and there is usually a selection of UK and foreign newspapers — all very expensive.

*Tradewinds* is published weekly on St. John in the high season, and monthly at other times, and is useful as it includes information about forthcoming events.

There are also many free newspapers and magazines widely available on the islands which give information about things to see and do, what's on and where to shop and dine.

The islands receive the full range of US cable and satellite channels via San Juan, and there are three local TV stations, and seven local radio stations, although many more, both English and Spanish speaking can be received.

## NIGHTLIFE

Things can get very lively after dark, and there are several nightspots, clubs and discos. Most hotels and many restaurants provide nightly live entertainment. In St. Thomas you can listen to jazz at Barnacle Bill's in Sub Base, disco at Walter's Living Room and Club Z in Charlotte Amalie, and dance at the Ritz. Also check out the Barbary Coast in Frenchtown, East Coast in Red Hook, and Raffles and Sugar's Niteclub, both in the capital. Most of the nightspots in St. Croix are in Christiansted, or restricted to hotels and restaurants in Frederiksted. Listen to steel bands at the Buccaneer Hotel, Hotel on the Cay and Carambola Beach Resort. In Christiansted there are Hondo's and the Wreck Bar nightclubs, and there are several venues for jazz, and folk music.

## PETS

Some airlines and many hotels do not accept pets and generally, it is not a good idea to take them with you if travelling from the US, as most pets will find the sudden heat of the tropics uncomfortable. If you must take your pet, it must have a certificate from a veterinary surgeon stating that it is disease-free, it comes from a rabies-free area, and has been vaccinated against rabies at least 30 days ago but within the last year, and its parvo virus shots are up to date.

Pets can be carried on board yachts and do not pose a problem provided they never come ashore.

## PHARMACIES

There are pharmacies in all towns on all islands.

## PHOTOGRAPHS

The intensity of the sun can play havoc with your films, especially if photographing near water or white sand. Compensate for the brightness otherwise your photographs will come out over exposed. The heat can actually damage film so store reels in a box or bag in the hotel fridge if there is one. Also remember to protect your camera if on the beach, as a single grain of sand is all it takes to jam your camera, and if left unprotected, it might 'disappear'. Always make sure when buying film that its expiry date is still a long way off.

It is very easy to get 'click

happy' in the Caribbean, but be tactful when taking photographs. Many islanders are shy or simply fed up with being photographed, and others will insist on a small payment. You will have to decide whether the picture is worth it, but if a person declines to have their photograph taken, do not ignore this. The islanders are a warm and very hospitable people, and if you stop and spend some time finding out what they are doing, they will usually then allow you to take a photograph. Film is quite expensive and it is better to take it with you, and carry spare batteries if your camera requires them, or change them for new ones just before departure.

## POST

Postage from the US. Virgin Islands is the same as on the mainland and a first class stamp costs 32c. All first class letters are sent air mail to the US mainland. Airmail postcards to the US cost 20c, and 40c to the UK and mainland Europe.

The main post office on St. Thomas is by Emancipation Park in Charlotte Amalie ☎ 774-1950. There are also post offices at Sugar Estate and on Veteran's Drive. On St. John the post office is in Cruz Bay, and on St. Croix there are post offices in the Customs House in Christiansted, in Richmond at La Reine, (Kingshill Centre), and at Mars Hill in Frederiksted.

## PUBLIC HOLIDAYS AND FESTIVALS

The islands enjoy 23 public holidays, more than almost anywhere else in the world, and most are excuses for parades and parties.

### January
January 1 — New Year's Day, Public Holiday. Children's costume parade in Frederiksted.

January 6 — Epiphany and Feast of the Three Kings Parade on St. Croix, which marks the end of the island's 12 days of celebration over Christmas.

January 15 — Martin Luther King Jr's Birthday - Public Holiday.

### February
February 20 — President's Day, Public Holiday (date can vary).
Agricultural Food Fair, St. Croix.

### March
Ash Wednesday

Memorial Day
St. Patrick's Day Parade, St. Croix.
Transfer Day, March 31.

## April

International Rolex Cup Regatta (early April).
Palm Sunday (date varies).
Good Friday (date varies).
Easter Sunday — and the start of a week of land and water-based sporting events, including the American Paradise Triathlon (dates vary).
Mid-Easter — the Rolex International Regatta.
Post-Easter — St. Thomas Carnival, several days of parades and partying.

## May

St. Croix International Triathlon.
May 29 — Memorial Day, Public Holiday (date varies).

## June

Whit Sunday — Pentecost.
Organic Act Day — Public Holiday (date varies).

## July

First week — St. John Carnival.
July 3 — Danish West Indies Emancipation Day.
July 4 — Independence Day, Public Holiday.
July 14 — Bastille Day, celebrated by French descendants on St. Thomas.
Hurricane Supplication Day — observed towards the end of the month in advance of the hurricane season.

## August

International Virgin Islands Atlantic Blue Marlin Tournament.
Atlantic Open Blue Marlin Tournament, St. Thomas.

## September

Labour Day — Public Holiday (date varies).

## October

October 9 — Columbus day, Public Holiday/Puerto Rico and Virgin Islands Friendship Day.
Hurricane Thanksgiving Day (date varies towards end of the month).
Sir Francis Drake Sail Race between St. Thomas and the British Virgin Islands.
International Mumm's Cup Regatta.

## November

November 1 — Liberty Day.
November 11 — Veterans' Day, Public Holiday.
November 23 — Thanksgiving, Public Holiday (date can vary).
Virgin Islands Charter Yacht Show.

Coral Bay Regatta — St. John.

## December

December 25 — Christmas Day, Public Holiday, start of St. Croix Christmas Fiesta which lasts until January 6.
December 26 — Second Christmas Day (Boxing Day), Public Holiday.
December 31 — New Year's Eve.

## SECURITY

St. Thomas and St. Croix do have a crime problem and it makes sense like anywhere else, not to walk around wearing expensive jewellery or flashing large sums of money. Extra care needs to be taken late at night, especially away from the centers of the larger towns, where street crime occasionally occurs. If out late at night, travel by taxi or with a crowd, and do not stray into unfamiliar, badly lit areas. It is a good idea to get a street map and familiarise yourself with it, learning the best way back to your hotel, not necessarily the quickest. Do not leave valuable items in unattended vehicles, or on the beach if going swimming.

Do not carry around your passport, travellers cheques or all your money. Keep them secure in your room or in a hotel safety deposit box. It is also a good idea to have photocopies of the information page of your passport, your air ticket and holiday insurance policy. All will help greatly if the originals are lost. Most hotels have their own security staff, but care should also be taken with valuables when by the pool and on the beach.

As with most tourist destinations, you might be pestered by touts trying to sell tours, souvenirs and even drugs, or by young people begging. A firm 'no' or 'not interested', is normally enough to persuade them to leave you alone.

Do not be alarmed at the large numbers of people who walk around with machetes. These are used throughout the island as a gardening implement.

## SPORTS
### Diving

There are dive centers and shops which hire all the necessary equipment. Instruction and training at all levels is also available, and boats can be chartered to visit offshore reefs and wrecks. Spearfishing is not allowed within the waters of the St. John National Park, but you are allowed to take up to two lobsters a day from the waters of the National Park, provided they are caught by hand, snare or pot, are not egg bearing, and have a tail at least 5½ inches (13.75cm) long.

Night diving is possible around all three islands. There is a decompression chamber on St. Thomas.

Best dive spots on St. Thomas are considered to be along the south coast. There are a number of safe shipwrecks to explore, such as the wrecks of the *Warrick* and 190ft (58m) freighter *Cartanser Senior* lying in 40ft (12m) of water near Packet Rock, and a plane wreck off the southwest coast. Best sites include: Armando's Reef, Capella Island, Coki Point, Cow and Calf Rocks, Dry Rocks, French Cap Cay, Inner Brass Island, Little St. James Reef, Sail Rock, Saba Island, Stevens Cay, the tunnels of Thatch Cay and the cays between St. Thomas and St. John.

Best dive sites off St. Croix include the coral and sponge encrusted Frederiksted Pier with its many species of tropical fish and seahorses. On the sea bed it is still possible to find coins and artifacts, some of them 300 years old. Other sites include David Bay, King's Reef, Salt River, West End Reef, and Buck Island where the water is rarely more than 12ft (4m) deep but visibility is 100ft (30m) and more. There is also The Pillar Coral where columns of coral up to 25ft (8m) high rise from the sandy ocean floor, North Cut, one of the tallest coral pinnacles in the Caribbean, and the Cane Bay Dropoff reached from the beach where the water rapidly deepens to more than 2,000ft (610m). In the Salt River estuary you can dive down a sheer cliff which plunges 1,000ft (305m) into the sea. There are 47 world-class dive sites around St. Croix.

On St. John, best sites include Coral Bay, Trunk Bay, Stevens Cay, Fishbowl Reef, Congo Bay and Carvel Rock.

Dive operators include:
**Anchor Dive Center**, Sunny Isle, St. Croix ☎ 778-1522 or 1-800-532-DIVE

**Aqua Action**, Red Hook, St. Thomas ☎ 775-6285

**Blue Dolphin Divers**, Sunny Isle, St. Croix ☎ 773-6834

**Cane Bay Dive Shop**, St. Croix ☎ 773-9913

**Caribbean Divers**, Red Hook, St. Thomas ☎ 775-6384

**Chris Sawyer Diving Center**, Frydenhoj, St. Thomas, ☎ 775-7320

**Cinnamon Bay Watersports**, St. John ☎ 776-6330

**Club St. Croix**, Christiansted, St. Croix ☎ 773-4800

**Coki Beach Dive Club**, Coral World, St. Thomas ☎ 775-4220

**Coral Bay Watersports**, Cruz Bay, St. John ☎ 776-6850

**Cruzan Divers**, Frederiksted, St. Croix ☎ 772-3701

**Cruz Bay Watersports**, Cruz Bay, St. John ☎ 776-6234

**Dive Experience**, Strand Street, Christiansted, St. Croix ☎ 773-3307

**DiveIn**, Sapphire Beach, St. Thomas ☎ 775-6100

**Dive St. Croix**, Kings Wharf ☎ 773-3434

**Hi-Tec Watersports**, St. Thomas ☎ 774-5650

**Joe Vogel Diving**, St. Thomas ☎ 775-7610

**Low Key Watersports**, St. John ☎ 776-7048

**Mile Mark Charters**, King's Wharf, Christiansted, St. Croix ☎ 773-2628

**Ocean Fantasies**, Windward Passage, St. Thoms ☎ 774-5223

**Ocean Quest Divers**, St. Thomas ☎ 777-7477

**St. John Watersports**, Cruz Bay, St. John ☎ 776-6256

**St. Thomas Diving Club**, Bolongo Bay, St. Thomas ☎ 776-2381

**Sea Adventures**, Frenchmen's Reef Beach Resort, St. Thomas ☎ 776-8500

**Underwater Safaris**, Green Cay Marina, St. Thomas ☎ 778-7350

**VI Divers**, Christiansted, St. Croix ☎ 773-6045

**Virgin Islands Diving School**, Vitraco Park, St. Thomas ☎ 774-8687

### Fishing

The waters around the Virgin Islands offer some of the best game and sport fishing in the world, and have resulted in many world records over the last few years, especially for blue and white marlin. Currently the islands have held 24 International Game Fish Association world records. Blue marlin weighing in at over 850lbs (382.5kg) have been caught, and the record stands at 1,282lbs (577kg). There is excellent year-round fishing for cobia, wahoo, kingfish, bonito, sailfish, marlin and allison. Most boats available for charter operate from Red Hook and East End Lagoon.

From March to June the blue marlin fishing is best to the south in the Caribbean, from July to September they start to move north, and from October to February, the best fishing is over the 6 mile (10km) deep Trench, the deepest part of the Atlantic Ocean.

**Best seasons are**: July to October for blue marlin, April to October for white marlin,

September to May for wahoo, April to September for yellowfish tuna, spring for dorado (dolphin), kingfish, and all year round for barracuda, snook, jack, grouper, tarpon and pompano.

**Some rules**: A recreational licence is not required if fishing with hand line, troll, cast net or snare. It is illegal to harm or kill turtles or their eggs, to remove or damage living coral, or to spearfish. There are catch and size limits for many game fish so be aware of the regulations before setting out.

Hotels, tour operators and the tourist offices can supply details about boats available for sea fishing charters.

Best fishing grounds are at Lang Bank off St. Croix, there is always good fishing off St. Thomas but the best grounds vary depending on the time of the year.

### Golf

**St. Thomas** — The 18-hole championship course at Mahogany Run, was designed by George and Tom Fazio as a par 70 ☎ 775-5000. Holes 13 and 14 run along the top of the cliffs so do not try and retrieve balls that go over!

**St. Croix** — There are two championship 18-hole courses. The course at the Carambola Resort ☎ 773-0747, was designed by Robert Trent Jones, and the other, designed by Bob Joyce, is at the Buccaneer Hotel ☎ 773-2100, and the Reef at Teague Bay Course ☎ 773-8844. There is a 9-hole course at the Reef.

### Horse Racing

There is racing on both St. Croix and St. Thomas, usually once a month and on Sundays or a public holiday.

### Horse Riding

There are the Paul and Jill's Riding stables at Estate Sprat Hall, Frederiksted (☎ 772-2880), and the Buccaneer Hotel, on St. Croix, at the Pony Express Riding Stables at Bordeaux Mountain on St. John (☎ 776-6494), and at the Rosenthal Riding Ring on St. Thomas (☎ 775-2636). Riding lessons and trail rides are available at all, and you can even go moonlight riding.

### Kayaking

Kayak rental is available on all three islands, and there are 5 and 7 day kayak tours of the British Virgin Islands from St. John with overnight camping.

### Power Boats

Motor boats are available for hire on all three islands, with or without a skipper. If you want to take the boat out alone, proof of previous experience is required.

### Surfing

The best surfing is on the north-eastern end of the island and along the Atlantic coast.

### Tennis

There are public and private courts on all three islands. Most of the large hotels and resorts have their own tennis courts, many of them floodlit. If you plan to play, try to get a court early in the morning or late in the afternoon for the first few days because of the midday sun, and do not play for too long until you get used to the heat.

### Water Sports

Every conceivable water sport is available on the islands from surfing and swimming to snorkelling and sailing, and water skiing to windsurfing (boardsailing). Best windsurfing on St. Thomas is at Cowpet, Vessup and Sapphire Beaches, and on St. John at Cinnamon Bay. Almost all hotels and resorts offer extensive watersport opportunities.

### Yachts

The waters around the islands attract yachts from around the world because of the excellent weather, calm waters and excellent anchorages, and the Virgin Islands play host to the largest charter fleet in the Caribbean. Scores of charter boats both bare board and crewed are available, from schooners and trimarans to power boats and small yachts, and there are many cruises to visit other islands. Crewed charters with everything included start from about $1200 per person a week. There are also several sailing schools where you can learn how to sail, in what must be one of the most exotic 'classrooms' in the world. World class racing events include the 3 day International Mumm's Cup Regatta, and the 3 day International Rolex Cup Regatta in April. Red Hook and Magens Bay are the bases for many of the charter boats. Yacht charter companies include:

**Bajor Yacht Charters**, St. Thomas ☎ 776-1954
**Big Beard's Adventure Tours, St. Croix** ☎ 773-4482
**Captain Heinz's Teroro 11**, Green Cay Marina,

Christiansted, St. Croix
☎ 773-3161
**Caribbean Yacht Charters**, St. Thomas ☎ 775-6003
**Easy Adventures**, Nazareth, St. Thomas ☎ 775-7870
**Junie Bomba's Sunset Cruises, Christainsted**, St. Croix ☎ 772-2482
**Llewellyn's Charter**, St. Croix ☎ 773-9027
**Mile Mark Charters**, King's Wharf, Christiansted, St. Croix ☎ 773-2285
**Terroro 11**, Green Cay Marina, St. Croix ☎ 773-3161
**Tropic Isles Yacht Charters**, St. John ☎ 776-6863
**Yacht Vacations**, St. Thomas ☎ 776-1666

Write to the Charter Yacht League, Hopeport, St. Thomas, United States Virgin Islands 00802 ☎ 774-3944 for information about charters.

## TAXES

There are no arrival or departure taxes, but there is a 7.5 per cent Government tax on all hotel rooms, and many hotels and restaurants also add a service charge of between 10 and 15 per cent. If this is added in a restaurant, there is no need to leave a tip, but in hotels, you may still want to leave a little extra for the room maid, who is unlikely to share in any of the added service charge.

## TAXIS

### St. Thomas
Dial-a-Ride ☎ 776-1277
East End Taxi Service ☎ 775-6974
Gainsway Taxi ☎ 775-9274
Gold Dust Taxi ☎ 773-0228
Golden Rock Taxi ☎ 778-7007
Independent Taxi Association ☎ 776-1006
Islander Taxi Service ☎ 774-4077
Sunshine Taxi Association ☎ 775-1145
VI Taxi Association ☎ 774-4550
Wheatley Taxi Service ☎ 775-1959

### St. John
Cool Running Taxis, Cruz Bay ☎ 774-7457
Hospitality Rent-a-Car, Cruz Bay ☎ 693-9160
St. John Taxi Association, Cruz Bay ☎ 776-6060

### St. Croix
Alphonso's Island Tour and Taxi ☎ 773-1031
Antilles Taxis ☎ 773-5020
Bright Star Taxi ☎ 773-3873
Caribbean Taxi Service and Tours ☎ 773-9799

Curzon Taxi and Tours
☎ 773-6388
Frederiksted Taxi and Tour
Service ☎ 772-4775
Hondos Corner Taxi
☎ 773-4220
St. Croix Taxi ☎ 778-1088
St. Croix Taxicab Association
☎ 778-1088
Transportation Unlimited
☎ 772-1512

## TELEPHONES

For calls to the US Virgin Islands from the United States dial 1-809 and the seven digit number. From the UK dial 001-1-809 and the seven digit number.

You can direct dial from the islands to the United States (1+area code+7 digit number), Canada and most countries world-wide (011+country code+area code+local number), and credit card calls can also be made. You can dial US AT&T Direct and other 800 numbers. The BT Direct operator number is 1 800 445 5667. For direct dial telephone 1 800 804 4826. Local calls cost 25c for each 5 minutes.

## TIME

The islands are on US Atlantic Standard Time which means that it is 1 hour ahead of Eastern Standard time. If it is 12noon in St. Thomas, it is 11am in Miami and New York, and the islands are 4 hours behind GMT, which means that if it is 12noon in London, it is 8am on St. Thomas.

## TIPPING

In restaurants it is usual to tip 15 per cent, or more for outstanding service, but always check to make sure service has not already been added to the bill. Tip taxi drivers 15 per cent on fixed fares, and 10 per cent on negotiated rates, but more if you think you got good service. Tip porters 50c to $1 for each item of luggage bag carried, and it is customary to leave a tip for your room maid, usually $1 for each night.

## TOURIST OFFICES

There are tourist information offices on St. Thomas in the airport arrivals terminal, at the West India Company cruise ship dock, and in the Grand Hotel lobby, Emancipation Square in Charlotte Amalie, and on St. Croix in the Old Scale House on the waterfront in Christiansted, and the Customs House in Frederiksted.

For more information write to:

**St. Thomas** — Box 6400, Charlotte Amalie, USVI 00801 ☎ 809-774-8748

**St. Croix** — Box 4538 Christiansted, USVI 00820 ☎ 809-773-0495

**St. John** - Box 200, Cruz Bay, USVI 00830 ☎ 809-776-6450

Tourist offices abroad

There are offices of the United States Division of Tourism in:

**Atlanta** — 235 Peachtree Center, Suite 1420, Gaslight Tower, Atlanta GA 30303 ☎ 404-688-0906.

**Chicago** — 1225 Michigan Avenue, Suite 1270 Chicago Il 60603 ☎ 312-461-0180

**Los Angeles** — 3450 Wiltshire Boulevard, Suite 915, Los Angeles CA 90010 ☎ 213-739-0138

**Miami** — 7270 NW 12th Street, Suite 620 Miami, Fl 33126 ☎ 305-591-2070

**New York** — 1270 Avenue of the Americas, New York NY 10020 ☎ 212-582-4520

**Washington** — 1667 K Street NW, Suite 270, Washington DC 20006 ☎ 293-3707

**Canada** - 3300 Bloor Street West, The Mutual Group Center, Suite 3120, Center Tower, Toronto ☎ 416-233-1414 or 1-800-465-8784

**UK**

US Department of Tourism, 2 Cinnamon Row, Plantation Wharf, York Place, London SW11 3TW ☎ 0171-978-5262

US Virgin Islands, 16 Bedford Square, London WC1B 3JA ☎ 0171-637-8481

## TOUR OPERATORS

There are many tour companies on the islands offering sightseeing trips, conducted walks, cruises and almost anything else you may want to do. Your hotel or the tourist information office can put you in touch with specialist tour operators, such as yacht, helicopter and aircraft charters.

**Caribbean Sea Adventures**, St. Croix ☎ 773-5922

Charles East-West Safari Tours, St. Croix ☎ 772-7236

Snorkelling Safari, St. Croix ☎ 773-0951

Southerland Tours, St. Croix ☎ 773-9500

St. Croix Safari Tours ☎ 773-6700

Travellers Tours, St. Croix ☎ 778-1636

## WATER

Drinking water from the tap is perfectly safe although bottled mineral and distilled water is widely available.

## WEDDINGS

Thousands of couples choose to marry on the islands, taking part in a barefoot sunset ceremony on the beach, one of the many hotel wedding gazebos, in church or at the Terrestrial Court. Getting married on the islands is so popular that there are even marriage planners and consultants who can help with all the details. Before choosing a planner, however, compare prices and what you will get for your money, and you can check their status with the Department of Licensing and Consumer Affairs ☎ 774-3130.

If you do not want a conventional wedding, how about getting married in Blackbeard's Castle or the St. Peter Greathouse Botanical Garden.

Apply for a marriage licence application to the Administrator, Territorial Court of the Virgin Islands, PO Box 70, St. Thomas 00801 ☎ 774-6680 if intending to marry on St. Thomas or St. John. If planning to marry on St. Croix, write to the Territorial Court of the Virgin Islands, Family Division, PO Box 929, Christiansted, St. Croix 00821 ☎ 778-9750.

If either party has been divorced, a certified copy of the divorce decree or a notarised affidavit stating when the divorce was granted must accompany the application. An 8 day waiting period is required after the completed and notarised application has been received by the court, but if you have a wedding consultant acting for you this can eliminate the need for an on-island waiting period.

If you want to be married by the Court, an appointment must be made for a Judge to perform the ceremony. Court marriages are performed by appointment on weekdays on St. Thomas and on Tuesday and Wednesday on St. Croix. There is a $25 application fee, the licence costs $25 and there is a $200 fee for being married by a Judge. For a church wedding, it is advisable to give the minister as much advance notice as possible.

There is a very useful booklet *Getting Married in the United States Virgin Islands* which tells prospective couples all they need to know. It is available from offices of the US Department of Tourism.

# Index

**A**
Administration 29
Altona Lagoon 124
Annaberg Plantation 87

**B**
Barents Bay 69
Batteriet Louise Augusta 124
Bolongo Beach 72
Bordeaux Bay 69
Bordeaux Mountain 88
Botany Bay 69
Brewers Bay 69
Buccaneer Beach 124
Buck Island Reef National Monument 125
Butler's Bay Greathouse 113

**C**
Cane Bay 112
Caneel Bay 85
Caneel Bay Plantation Resort 85
Canegarden Bay 129
Carambola Resort 113
Charlotte Amalie (St. Thomas) 10, 47, 48-68
   Atlantis Submarine 64
   Bethania Hall 53
   Blackbeard's Castle 57
   Bluebeard's Castle 64
   Camille Pissarro Building 60
   Danish Consulate 64
   Emancipation Park 53
   Enid M. Baa Library 60
   Fort Christian 52
   Fort Cowell (Hassel Island) 61
   Frederick Lutheran Church 56
   Frederik Lutheran Church Parsonage 57
   Government House 56
   Grand Hotel 53
   Hotel 1829 10, 57
   Legislature Building 52
   Main Street 60
   Market 60
   Old Cable Building 56
   Paradise Point Tramway 64
   Post Office 53
   Seven Arches Museum 56
   Signal Hill 64
   St. Thomas Reformed Church 59
   St. Thomas Sephardic Synagogue 59
   Street of 99 Steps 57
   Tourist Office 53
   Vendors Plaza 52
Chenay Bay 125
Chenay Bay Beach Resort 125
Christiansted (St. Croix) 10, 101-110
   'Alexander Hamilton' House 105
   Apothecary Hall 104
   Customs House 103
   Estate Grange 108
   Florence A. Williams Library 105
   Fort Christianvaern 103
   Friedensthal Moravian Church 108
   Government House 105
   Lord God of Sabaoth Lutheran Church 105
   Mahogany Inn 104
   Market Place 104
   Markoe House 104
   Post Office 103
   Protestant Cay 108
   Scale House 102
   St. John's Anglican Church 105, 108
   Steeple Building 104
Cinnamon Bay 87
Cinnamon Trail 87
Coakley Bay 125
Coki Beach 74
Coki Point 74
Compass Point 72
Coral Bay 89
Coral World 10, 74
Cowpet Bay 73
Cramer Recreation Park 128
Cruz Bay (St. John) 81-85
   Battery 84
   Elaine Sprauve Library and Estate Catrineberg 84
   St. John Museum 84
   Moravian Bethany Mission 84
   National Park Visitor's Center 81
Culture 26

**D**
Davis Bay 113
Drake's Seat 77
Drink 45
Drunk Bay 92

**E**
East End Bay 92
Economy 28
Elk Bay 92
Estate Carolina 92
Estate Great Pond 128
Estate Lameshur 88
Estate St. Peter Greathouse and Botanical Gardens 69
Estate Tutu 74

**F**
Fairchild Park 70
Fairleigh Dickinson University's West Indies Laboratory 126
Flora & Fauna 30
Food 41
Fortuna Bay 69
Francis Bay 87
Frederiksted (St. Croix) 10, 115-124
   Benjamin House 116
   Betty's Hope 120
   Container Port 121
   Cruzan Rum Distillery 120

## INDEX

Customs House 115
Fleming Building 116
Fort Frederik 115
Friedensborg Moravian Mission 117
Holy Trinity Lutheran Church 117
Long Point Bay 120
Old Apothecary Hall 116
Old Danish School 117
Old Library 116
Old Market 117
St. Croix Aquarium 116
St. Patrick's Roman Catholic Cathedral Church 117
St. Paul's Episcopal Church 117
Tourist Information Center 115
Victoria House 116
French Town 68
Frenchman's Cap 72
Friis Bay 92

### G
Gallows Bay 124
Geography 9
Grapetree Beach 128
Great Bay 73
Great Lameshur Bay 92
Great Salt Pond Bay 128
Grootpan Bay 92

### H
Hansen Bay 92
Haulover 92
Hawksnest Beach 85
History 13
Hull Bay 69
Hurricane Hole 92

### I
Isaac Point 128
Island Center 121

### J
John's Foly Bay 92
Johnson Bay 92
Judith Fancy 110
Jumbie Bay 87

### K
Kiddel Bay 92

### L
Lameshur Bay 89
Long Bay 92

### M
Magens Beach & Bay 10, 76
Maho Bay 87
Mahogany Run Golf Course 76
Manchenil Bay 129
Mandal Bay 76
Mennebeck Bay 92
Morningstar Bay 72
Mountain Top 70

### N
Nazareth Bay 73
Newfound Bay 92

### O
Off The Wall, Cane Bay 10, 112

### P
Pelican Cove 110
People, the 25
Perseverence Bay 69
Point Udall 128
Port Hess 121
Privateer Bay 92
Punnett Point 125

### R
Rainbow Beach 115
Ram Head 92
Redhook Harbor 73
Reef Golf Course 125
Reichhold Center for the Performing Arts 68
Round Bay 92

### S
Salomon Bay 85
Salt River Bay 112
Saltpond Bay 92
Sandy Bay 69
Sandy Point 117
Sapphire Bay 74
Sauteurs 10
Secret Harbor Bay 73
Shoy Beach 125
Skyline Drive 77
Solitude Bay 125
Sprat Hall 113
Sprat Hall Beach 113
Sprat Hall Plantation 113
ST. CROIX 20, 100-129
St. Croix Leap 113
St. Croix Yacht Club 125
St. Croix-by-the-Sea 110
St. George Botanical Garden 10, 120, 129
St. George Village 120
ST. JOHN 17, 80-100
St. Peters' Mount 69-80
ST. THOMAS 16, 48-80
Stony Ground 117
Stouffer Renaissance Grand Beach Resort 74
Stumpy Bay 69

### T
Tague Bay 125
Thatch Cay 74
Trunk Bay 10, 87
Trunk Beach 87

### U
US National Park Service Headquarters 73

### V
Virgin Islands Ecological Research Station 92

### W
Weather 24
Whim Greathouse 117